Sassy Godmother's
Pearls of Wisdom

Sassy Godmother's
Pearls of Wisdom

*50 inspiring ways
to navigate your life*

SUSIE HALL

T

The manufacturer's authorised representative in the EU
for product safety is Authorised Rep Compliance Ltd,
71 Lower Baggot Street, Dublin D02 P593 Ireland (www.arccompliance.com)

Troubador Publishing Ltd
Unit E2 Airfield Business Park,
Harrison Road, Market Harborough,
Leicestershire. LE16 7UL
Tel: 0116 2792299
Email: books@troubador.co.uk
Web: www.troubador.co.uk

ISBN 978-1-83628-472-7

British Library Cataloguing in Publication Data.
A catalogue record for this book is available from the British Library.

Printed and bound in Great Britain by 4edge Limited
Typeset in 11pt Adobe Garamond Pro by Troubador Publishing Ltd, Leicester, UK

This book is dedicated to the loving memory of Ann Smith
Known affectionately to me as A.A.

My own beloved godmother

"Information is just bits of data.
Knowledge is putting them together.
Wisdom is transcending them."
RAM DASS
SPIRITUAL TEACHER AND WRITER

Why read this book?

Let's face it. This life you're leading can be bloody hard at times, can't it? It's way more complicated and potentially confusing than it ever used to be. It's more competitive, it's loud, it's busy and it's full of information that you have to deal with on a daily basis. And the world we're currently living in is unpredictable and sometimes scary. And that can bring with it a lot of stress and angst. If you feel you need a bit of a reboot, you want to take a deep breath and a good hard look at what you're doing and why, this is the book for you.

It's also the book for you if you're curious. If you actually want to *thrive* rather than just exist. If you want to make your life richer and make it flow more easily. If you want to show up fully and confidently as yourself.

These Pearls of Wisdom are a distillation of my life's observations, lessons, fuck-ups and experiences as well as the experiences of the many hundreds of clients I've worked with. I've sought out inspiring teachers who've helped me to understand more about life's mysteries. Hundreds of books, courses, talks and travels to work out how to get the most out of this extraordinary human experience of ours. I've experimented with all kinds of tools and techniques to enrich my life and I've done some pretty weird and scary shit along the way.

And then it occurred to me. Why not pass this wisdom on to you, so you can learn from my journey to enrich yours? If you can embrace some of these Pearls of Wisdom now, chances are your life will become more interesting, fulfilling and less anxious. You'll reap the rewards if you want to grow and shape your life differently. Because I haven't written this as food for thought. I've written it so you can take *action*. And that's probably going to be challenging. I want to get you thinking about your life and why you're here. I want to plant some seeds in that wonderfully curious mind of yours. I want to inspire and empower you so you can change your life in whatever way feels right for you.

How to get the most out of this book

This book is an amalgamation of wisdom. So I suggest you look at it as a *smorgasbord*. I do love that word. A buffet-style selection of wisdom that you can dip in and out of and come back to again and again, depending on what's going on in your life. You could start by skimming through the book and taking note of the areas that really resonate with you. And *then* you can dig a whole lot deeper. Or because of how you roll, you might want to work through it systematically, Pearl by Pearl.

For each Pearl of Wisdom, I've given you a short memorable mantra. This is to remind you what to do when you're facing a challenging situation. I want you to imagine I'm sitting on your shoulder gently encouraging you. Many of my coaching clients have had me sitting on their shoulders when the shit hits the fan. I pop up to remind them what we talked about and what they promised they'd do when whatever it was happened.

Each Pearl has what I call Actionable Advice. This is the practical stuff. What you could do or say differently, how to approach situations, what to look out for, tips and tools to make life easier. These are immediately applicable and straightforward. And some of the Pearls have resources marked with a * if you want to delve a little deeper. These are my suggestions of books, websites, talks, clips, individuals and organisations who might be useful to you. And you can find them at the back of the book.

Then at the end of every Pearl, there are some Actions and Considerations. This is space for you to do some self-reflection and journalling. I've asked you questions to get you thinking and give you further insights so you can take action. You might want to take the time to do this before moving on to the next Pearl.

Some Pearls will be obvious to you, and some you'll find more challenging than others. You can keep returning to your Considerations and look back at how your thoughts, feelings and behaviours have changed over time.

So what are we going to talk about?

The first step of our journey together is getting to know your sweet self better.

> *"Awareness is the greatest agent for change."*
> **ECKHART TOLLE, SPIRITUAL TEACHER**
> **AND SELF-HELP AUTHOR**

Being aware of who you are has been **THE** great spiritual quest for thousands of years. And there's always been much debate in philosophical circles about who actually coined the phrase "know thyself". It's scrawled in stone in the Temple of Apollo in Delphi. But suffice it for you and I to agree it was some wise old Greek guy who had a pretty good handle on the human psyche.

As far as you're concerned, *self-awareness* is the first step on your path to growth. Being able to understand what makes you tick, how you react under certain circumstances, how you come across to others, what you want, where your strengths and natural tendencies lie as well as understanding your blind spots and shadows, will give you the clues to being a more confident and fuller version of yourself. "Being authentic" has become a bit of an overused term but it is very important. I prefer to talk about you finding your "True Nature" which is a slightly bigger concept, but one I believe is your ultimate quest. When you find your True Nature, your life will flow more easily. You'll stop fighting life and be more in alignment with it. And by discovering and using your strengths and superpowers, you can give your gifts to others and be of service. I believe that's one of the major reasons we're all here.

Along the way, you're going to encounter some bumps in the road. In fact, from time to time you'll hit some massive great roadblocks. So building *self-mastery* is an important part of your journey and your skill set. And in trying to be the best version of yourself, you'll inevitably encounter resistance both from yourself and from others who don't like the direction you're taking. They may struggle with the new you or the different way you're behaving and being. A good dollop of self-mastery will help you to overcome the resistance to change. It'll give you the means to stand up for what you believe in and for who you are.

We'll also talk about the way you show up at work and manage your career. Navigating the world of work can be tricky whatever field you're in. It's still a patriarchy in many ways, both in its structure and culture. We need women working together to make the necessary changes. And you shouldn't have to turn yourself into a man to operate in a man's world.

So let's make a start, shall we?

Let this wisdom guide you. See me as your coach, mentor and chief cheerleader.

Your Sassy Godmother
X

PEARL 1

....

Be your own best friend

> *"We have to learn to be our own best friends because we fall too easily into the trap of becoming our own worst enemies."*
> *RODERICK THORP, NOVELIST*

This is where you begin. And you might accuse me of stating the bleeding obvious, but I'm going to say it anyway. The most important relationship you're ever going to have with anyone is with *yourself*. It all starts with you. To show up fully in the world, you need to know and understand yourself. And you need to build a healthy relationship with yourself. How you *interact* with yourself, how you *talk* to yourself and how you *treat* yourself are fundamental to the relationships you're going to have with the rest of the world. How you view yourself will define what you get out of life.

> *"How you love yourself is how you teach others to love you."*
> *RUPI KAUR, POET, ILLUSTRATOR, PHOTOGRAPHER AND AUTHOR*

1

For example, if you're always putting other people first because you have a certain view of yourself and you want to please others more, you may end up feeling unhappy and resentful because actually the wiser part of you knows it just isn't good for you.

You need to be able to understand more about how you function and why you behave the way you do. What works well for you and what doesn't? What triggers you? What beliefs do you hold? The frightening thing is you've actually got no idea why you do most of what you do. You're operating on autopilot most of the time. According to what you've always done. Or always thought. So let's shine a light on this and make you more *conscious*.

> *"When you try to understand everything, you will not understand anything. The best way is to understand yourself, and then you will understand everything."*
> *SHUNRYU SUZUKI, ZEN MONK*
> *AND TEACHER*

Actionable advice

One of the easiest ways to get to know anyone is to hang out with them more. The problem is, the society we live in doesn't really encourage you to do this. There's far more emphasis on the external rather than the internal. The way we live now doesn't promote solitude, silence or stillness.

It's all about noise, busyness, constant movement and short attention spans. But that's not going to help you understand yourself more. Or build a better relationship with yourself. That's why lockdown was a positive time for some people and utter hell for others. Because they were stuck with themselves. So you've got to make a real effort to carve out some time to just hang with yourself a bit more often. Listen to what's going on inside. Just sit with what comes up from all those external exchanges you have with everyone either face to face or virtually. That way you can start to hear the inner chatter and observe your thoughts.

Do you have a voice inside your head? Sometimes this voice can make unhelpful comments. The inner critic can come from a variety of places. It can be your own harsh judge or perfectionist, compounded by other people's opinions about you which you've sucked up as the truth. If your critic is so loud and so frequent, it can become debilitating. I've seen people apologizing constantly for just existing, trying to alter their personality to fit in with what they think their partner, friends or work colleagues want. Some of my clients have felt unworthy of compliments, praise or love. If you recognise even a glimmer of this within you, it's high time we reassess the relationship you have with yourself.

Start by becoming more conscious of what your inner voice is saying. Actually capturing the language you use when you talk to yourself and the beliefs you're holding on to is the first part of this journey. I'd even suggest you write it down. This will help you to understand what kind of conversation is going on inside your head. Do this for a week and see what you come up with.

Journalling is a good way of spending time with yourself. It doesn't have to be a big arduous task and another thing to add to your to-do list. It can be five minutes of quiet, reflective time first thing in the morning or last thing at night, depending on whether you're a lark or an owl. Sometimes just allowing your mind to wander and reflect on the day's events is a lovely practice. I don't even go back and read my journal. It's a cathartic exercise to get out my thoughts and opinions, frustrations, challenges and ideas. Just write it out and then let it go. It's not about perfect English or even making sense. This is for your eyes only. Just write to get some clarity on things. Or to admit there's no clarity. It doesn't matter.

And when you screw up, what happens? Do you beat yourself up and give yourself a hard time? If that's the case, we need to work on a new script. Think about what you might say differently. I tend to treat myself like a friend who's being a bit of a muppet. With compassion, love and humour. I try to ask myself the questions, "What did I learn from that?" "How would I do that differently next time?" and "How could I have phrased that differently?"

We all have an inner critic who shows up from time to time. It's just that some people have a louder and more persistent one than others. But just remember you have an inner cheerleader, too. Your supportive and encouraging self. How often do you praise yourself? How about congratulating yourself when you execute a cool parking manoeuvre or arrange some flowers nicely or complete some IT wizardry? It could be something really small, but still pat yourself on the back. I'd love you to try this. It's not big-headed, it's not arrogant and it's not narcissistic. It's just an acknowledgement of something you've done well. Like you'd say to a friend or partner. Just take one day. For one day notice the good stuff you've done and say something to acknowledge yourself. If you really want to go for it, give yourself a hug. See how *that* feels. Might feel weird. Might feel spectacular! One day. Can you do that for me? For yourself?

> "You yourself, as much as anybody in the entire universe, deserve your love and affection."
> BUDDHA, RELIGIOUS TEACHER

Just tune in and allow that voice to be heard and to cheer more loudly. Just like the rest of us, there's a part of you that's a little kid stuck in an adult body. The trick is to honour that child by helping it navigate the world outside rather than constantly criticising and being mean to it. As much as you'd want someone else to come and hold you with kindness and compassion, you need to be able to do this for yourself. You need to be your own best friend. Some of my clients have told me they just tell their inner critic to fuck off. Which I totally get. If you had a friend who constantly said you were crap, said you weren't good enough, was harsh and mean you probably would want to tell them to eff off. But that part of us reacts like that because It's *scared*. It needs firmly reassuring. It needs love. Talking to yourself like you would to someone you love is what I'd recommend you do instead. It takes a level of self-awareness and practice not to automatically beat yourself up, but do it regularly enough and it will become a new habit. A wonderful new habit.

Let me introduce you to a Buddhist concept called *maitri*,* pronounced *may-tree*. Maitri is benevolence. A loving kindness and genuine care for every individual. But maitri also applies to showing loving kindness to oneself. Which, as we all know, is a lot harder. But this is what you need to learn to do. Maitri is knowing you have flaws, you make mistakes, you aren't perfect, you are a messy, loveable human being. And you're *still* worthy of whatever goodness comes your way. Just because. Being able to embrace *all* of yourself with acceptance and a degree of self-love and even humour rather than harsh criticism, is a great practice to start.

ACTION/CONSIDERATION

Monitor your inner voice for a week.

What is the vibe of the voice? Is it mean and critical or encouraging and patient?

What language does it use?

Where in your life could you ease up on yourself a bit?

When you think about spending time alone just with yourself, how does it make you feel?
Can you identify why?

If you were able to carve out a short amount of quiet reflective time for yourself, when would work for you?

PEARL 2

....

Understand the difference between self-care and self-love

> *"Self-love is an ocean and your heart is a vessel. Make it full, and any excess will spill over into the lives of the people you hold dear. But you must come first."*
> *BEAU TAPLIN, AUTHOR*

We hear a lot about self-care these days. And yes, self-care is absolutely important. Hey, I'm the original spa queen. I've had every kind of massage under the sun. Hot stones, oil on my forehead, blind monks in Thailand digging into my ribs, two people at once (that's not what I meant). Massages with crystals, massages with coffee, massages with chocolate, the list is endless. Bubble baths, walks in nature, quiet time away from the tech or the kids, spending fun time with a partner or the girls, doing something creative. *All* good. Absolutely. But, I want you to understand the difference between that *external* stuff and the *internal* work of building self-love.

The two are very different.

It's no good spending a fortune on beauty products, vitamin supplements, gym memberships and God knows what else the "wellness" industry throws at you, if your mental health is in tatters. You can buy self-care and indulge in the pleasurable activities that relax and rejuvenate you. But you can't buy self-love. Don't confuse the two. The famous beauty brand that told you to spend your money on their products "because you're worth it" was trying to tell you that you could buy self-esteem. Which, of course, is bollocks. Self-love is a much deeper concept. It's not about advertising slogans. It's about deep self-respect and having boundaries because you genuinely care about yourself and how you're treated. Self-love is not narcissistic. You have to build it, practise it and nurture it. It takes work and it takes time. It's an ongoing journey that lasts your whole life. The good news is that you become a stronger, less anxious and happier human. This is about building the kind of relationship with yourself that enables you to deal with what the world throws at you. Everyone needs to do it. But most people don't. And *it's not because you're broken or you need fixing.* Everyone needs to build self-love and self-acceptance. It's part of being more resilient to the shit the world throws at you.

When my dad was in the latter stages of his dementia, he was looked after by live-in carers. I had to explain to the carers that the tap in the kitchen sink must be kept in the centre at all times, otherwise Dad would get stressed. They thought it was mildly amusing and there was a part of me that found it mildly irritating. And never more so than a few years later when I found myself doing precisely the same thing! WTF?

And having to pick up bits off the carpet. Really? Mild OCD obviously runs in the family. My uncle and cousin have the same. I was at an event in London where Elizabeth Gilbert (she of *Eat, Pray, Love*) was doing a talk. She walked amongst the audience with the microphone, asking us what we needed to give ourselves permission to do. I grabbed the mic and loudly proclaimed, "Stop picking bits off the fucking carpet." This was met with hoots of laughter. But since then, I've learned a valuable lesson. It's part of who I am. It's what makes me reasonably efficient, clean, tidy and house proud. My partner is quite used to putting the plug back in the centre of the taps because that's the way I like it. It's been an important journey of self-acceptance. Rather than finding it irritating or shameful, I tend to treat it with gentle-natured humour, preferring to focus on the positive aspects of it rather than the irrational ones. Is the world going to fall apart if all the kitchen surfaces aren't clean? Of course not. I know that rationally – I just prefer it that way. (And it goes without saying that if the OCD becomes life limiting, it's probably time to seek professional help.)

Actionable advice

So how do you build self-love and acceptance? Remember we talked about maitri? By turning your attention inwards and sitting with yourself and listening and observing. Your ability to forgive and accept yourself is a key part of you learning to love yourself more. This is all part of building inner resilience and confidence. Loving yourself when you're happy and confident is one thing. Being able to love yourself when you screw up, or when you're angry or sad is another. But by being softer with yourself and not beating yourself up, by treating yourself like you'd treat someone you deeply love and care for, you might start to make different decisions about what you'll tolerate from others. If their behaviour is damaging or harmful to you, you'll start to protect yourself like you'd protect someone you really love. Like you're protecting your inner child. Imagine how you love your partner, husband, wife, boy/girlfriend, your parents. This is the extent and depth of love that you need to turn inwards to yourself. Maitri is about taking a torch and lighting up the parts of you that you don't like.

The term "shadow side" was first coined by the Swiss psychoanalyst Carl Jung. Your shadow is all the bits of you that you find unacceptable, shameful, yukky and weak. Jung reckoned that you need to be able to see and accept this shadow side of yourself to be a fully integrated and balanced human being.

> *"Who looks outside, dreams; who looks inside, awakes."*
> CARL JUNG, PSYCHIATRIST
> AND PSYCHOANALYST

And I'm inclined to agree with the old boy. What's interesting is that most people see the "shadow" as something negative. In fact, the shadow can be hugely beneficial. Sadness can help you be more compassionate towards others, whilst anger can help you set stronger boundaries. The important thing is to understand and accept your "flaws". If you can do that, you'll be able to understand and accept others much more easily. I have much more empathy nowadays with people who exhibit the same OCD tendencies that I do, rather than getting impatient with them. I get it. Once you build a kinder relationship with your own foibles and shortcomings, you'll become a lot more compassionate and patient with other people's "irritating" habits. This is a great way of improving your relationships with both yourself and others.

The other thing about the shadow side is the mirror effect. What you don't like in others is often a reflection of the things you don't like about yourself. What really pisses you off about other people? How does that stack up with the shadow parts of yourself?

I find other people's selfishness hugely irritating. I have to keep reminding myself it's triggering something in me. Otherwise it wouldn't bother me in the slightest that people put their feet on the seats on trains, talk loudly in quiet coaches and leave their litter everywhere. And as for Range Rover drivers… don't get me started…

ACTION/CONSIDERATION

What one simple thing could you do to start a practice of self-love, as opposed to self-care?

Which bits of you do you find difficult?

Which bits are you ashamed of or embarrassed about? List them out and sit with them. Then take them one by one and just reflect on each of them with an attitude of acceptance and integration.

How could those aspects of yourself be of service to you?

PEARL 3

....

Live with intention

> *"Life isn't about finding yourself.*
> *Life is about creating yourself."*
> **GEORGE BERNARD SHAW, PLAYWRIGHT,**
> **CRITIC AND POLITICAL ACTIVIST**

I believe you have the potential to *continuously create* the life
you want, rather than passively accepting the current hand of
cards you've been dealt. I've long held the view that my life's
a glorious project and I'm its chief architect. If I don't like the
look of what I've created, I have the power to tear up the plans
and start again. And so do you.

We can be guilty of sleepwalking through our lives, acting
on autopilot and doing the same old things because that's
what we've always done. I call that *living unintentionally*.
And it often takes something drastic like the death of
someone close to you or something unexpected like Covid
for us to wake up, take a step back and reset or even create,
our *intention*.

> *"Your present circumstances don't determine where you can go; they merely determine where you start."*
> *NIDO QUBEIN, AMERICAN LEBANESE BUSINESSMAN AND PRESIDENT OF HIGHPOINT UNIVERSITY*

Having an explicit conscious intention is useful to give your inner architect some clue as to how to start shaping and changing your life. If you can be more intentional, it will help you act with more purpose, focus and more conviction. It'll stop you drifting aimlessly through life with no clear idea of what you want or where you're going. And it will help you to make better decisions.

So what do I mean by the intention of your life?

We're going to talk later about following your North Star, which I see as your *short-term* goals and projects. The *intention* for your life is something far bigger, grander and longer term. I'll tell you mine and then you'll get the drift. My intention is "to follow my True Nature, be of service, whilst keeping peace of mind and having fun".

So, in other words, I'm aiming to realise the potential I've been given, help others wherever I can, not get too stressed and have a lot of fun in the process. These are the principles of intention around which I live, how I choose to work, play, spend my money and my time. For example, my meditation time every day is non-negotiable. The desire to maximise my potential and be of service to others will guide me in the kind of work I choose to do and the way I give back to community. Is this helping me to grow? Yes or No? Am I changing people's lives for the better? Is this work enjoyable? Do I enjoy working in this kind of environment with these people? Let me tell you, as I've got older seeking out fun and joy has become a key part of my intention. If this resonates with you, don't wait til you get to my age to prioritise this in your life. I've turned down working with some types of companies because they were so up their own arses, took themselves far too seriously and thought they were doing me a favour.

Meh.

Actionable advice

If you feel you've lost focus or you've been through a period of enormous change and need a reboot, it might be time to take a step back and have a good hard look at the various aspects of your life.

I did precisely that a few years ago and it was genuinely life-changing. After leaving my marriage, moving house and area, losing my dad and changing how I worked (Jesus, no wonder I lost weight), I decided to do an online personal development process called Lifebook.* Once you get over the slightly schmaltzy American delivery, the programme really is very professionally put together and I'd highly recommend it to you. It helps you to examine pretty much every area of your life and think about what you want and why and how you're going to make it happen.

We went through the whole shebang... my Character, Health and Fitness, Intellectual and Emotional Life, Love and Social Life, Spiritual Life, Finances, Career and overall Quality of Life, looking at the beliefs I had for each one. What an interesting process *that* was!

I then looked at my Vision, Purpose and Strategy for each category, which helped me to make the changes I needed to get back in alignment with my intention. I subsequently joined a gym, started doing yoga again, hired a nutritionist, joined a dating site, stopped the work I wasn't enjoying and started writing. As it turned out, the repercussions were *massive*.

I'm a "whole hog" kinda gal, so every now and again I tend to chuck everything up in the air and start again. That approach clearly isn't for everyone and I was lucky and in a position to be able to make some major changes. Your imagination has been called "The Scissors of the Mind", constantly cutting and shaping the pattern of your life. You *do* have the power to create it in every moment with what you can control. If you decide to. I know at some points in your life there'll be big changes you want to make and at others it'll only be possible to make smaller tweaks. If you're a working mum with small children, your life is going to be full on. Reading this, you might think "yeah right, when do I have time to do *that*?" But don't give up creating *your* life because you have little ones or elderly parents to look after. You can still work on *something*. However small that is. Don't let "the scissors" cut *you* completely out of the picture. The point of this is to remind you how important *your* intention is. It's so easy to lose yourself when you're looking after others. Keep looking at your life and seeing where you can make positive changes, tweaks and improvements to align with that intention.

ACTION/CONSIDERATION

If you were to think of the intention for your life, what would that be?

When you think about making changes to your life, what are the first things that come to mind?

What do you want and why?

PEARL 4

....

Discover and follow your True Nature

When I talk about your "True Nature", I believe there's a strong spiritual aspect to it. My sense is that there's a part of us all that's been created from some kind of Divine Intelligence or Source. Some people call this the Soul. And then there's another part of us which is our personality. This contains all the gifts, abilities and "tendencies" towards things – music, maths, art, communication, sport, whatever it is, that's ***totally unique to you***. So your *True Nature* is a combination of your Soul and your personality. I think part of your journey is to get back to your True Nature.

I was talking to a client recently who wanted to raise her profile with some senior stakeholders within her business. This is what she told me. "When I'm in some senior meetings, I'm surrounded by lots of big personalities who dominate. They talk a lot with loud voices but I'm an introvert and a reflector. What happens is I feel bad for not speaking up. So I end up saying something for the sake of it, which has no real impact. And I think that's damaging people's perception of me."

My client felt like *she* should change herself. So we knocked that idea on the head straight away. The introvert/extrovert split is one of the most basic elements of your personality and short of developing a personality disorder, introverts don't suddenly change into extroverts.

Actionable advice

My client was visibly relieved when I reassured her that she didn't have to change herself. We just needed to work on giving her some strategies to manage herself and her perception in a slightly different way. If you know you're more introverted, it's about managing your brand so people start to see your introvert qualities as valuable strengths rather than weaknesses. There's huge power in a quiet, reflective and thoughtful approach.* But *you* need to recognise and see them as valuable strengths first. You need to accept, embrace and yes, celebrate, your uniqueness.

> *"Tension is who you think you should be.*
> *Relaxation is who you are."*
> **CHINESE PROVERB**

You may feel pressure to conform. This seems far greater now and can be driven by certain "celebrities" or influencers. I have to say, I've always favoured style over fashion and I've never wanted to look like anyone else. On the contrary.

> *"I think the reward for conformity is that*
> *everyone likes you except yourself."*
> **RITA MAE BROWN, FEMINIST WRITER**

Something else which can stop you finding your way back to your True Nature is comparing yourself to others. One of the biggest differences now compared to when I was younger, is the impact of social media. You're exposed to everyone else's lives in a way I never was. You're constantly bombarded, *if you choose to be*, by what others are buying, wearing, eating, drinking, thinking.

And of course, some of it's interesting, informative, inspiring and motivating. But social media has made "comparison" a very real feature of everyday life. Comparing your inner world which, like most of us, can be a bloody mess sometimes, to someone else's carefully curated outer shiny "successful" show reel, can make you stressed and unhappy. Thinking that everyone else is constantly living the dream, has life nailed, is supremely confident all the time, and is better than you, is *extremely damaging*. As well as being utter bollocks. Everyone suffers, everyone has issues and challenges and dark moments. We're human. It goes with the territory. We're all simply muddling along, doing the best we can. Some people just go to great lengths to avoid showing any vulnerability or any aspect of their lives that are not shiny and wonderful. Which is unrealistic.

Part of following your True Nature is finding what your "craft" or tendency is. And it might not happen straight away. Not finding a true vocation or purpose can be a source of much angst for many people. But not everyone knows they want to be a doctor or a pilot when they leave school or university. In fact, I'd say that's the exception rather than the rule. There's a part of you that knows. And you'll get glimpses of it from time to time. Because it's where you feel comfortable and things just flow easily and where you enjoy what you're doing and it plays to your natural strengths. And sometimes it can scare the living shit out of you because it might be so far away from where you are now. I've seen people start to question their careers in their late twenties and thirties. Maybe because it wasn't actually *their* choice to be a doctor, a lawyer, a finance professional or a surveyor. Maybe it was their parents' or it came from peer pressure. Or it seemed like "a good idea at the time". And it might be a gradual process to work your way "back" to your natural craft.

> *"Can you remember who you were, before the world told you who you should be?"*
> **CHARLES BUKOWSKI, POET AND NOVELIST**

And if you're really not sure if you're on the right path in the work you're doing, think twice before you over-leverage yourself. Once you've got the massive mortgage and the kids at private school, it's so much harder to make a U-turn. I've seen so many people fall into that trap.

But the good news is, what I've noticed over the years about following your True Nature, or your heart, is that it seems your *commitment gets rewarded*. Somehow, some way, when you step on to the path of your True Nature it's as if you align yourself more closely with what I call the Universal Mind (you might call it something else). And magical things show up. It's happened to me on a number of occasions and I've witnessed it in others multiple times. I've seen people change career and follow their hearts and suddenly "out of nowhere" comes huge fulfilment and financial reward. I used to think it was coincidence but I've long since given up believing that. There's something going on here and I want you to understand this.

I used to describe this process using "angels" as a metaphor for the Univeral Mind. There were a group of angels somewhere in the dimension where angels hang out and they were playing a game of poker. From time to time, they'd look down on me and see what I was up to. I was carrying on doing what I was doing. I wasn't being courageous or following my heart. But when I finally decided I'd follow my intuition and commit to some courageous action, they put their cards down and came and helped me.

> *"If you are on the right path you will find*
> *that invisible hands are helping."*
> **JOSEPH CAMPBELL, WRITER**

I knew I was unhappy in my marriage. It was tricky because my husband is a lovely man – we were just heading in different directions. It took me several years to be able to summon not only the courage, but the finances to fund a deposit and rent on a new home. I was working with a coach at the time (David, you're wonderful) who came up with a very bold plan which scared the shit out of me. He suggested that I put a proposal together to one of my corporate clients for a 6-month retainer arrangement, shared by two heads of department and payable in advance. I thought it was an audacious idea but knew I needed to do something. If they accepted, it would mean I could make the move and start a new life. I put on my big girl pants, made the proposal and guess what? They accepted and the money landed in my bank account not long after. The speed at which things happened was nothing short of miraculous. I believe this is the Universal Mind in action.

Following your True Nature requires you to pay attention to how you're feeling and to follow your intuition. Part of you knows if you're a square peg in a round hole and you're in the wrong place, job, relationship or house. If this is you, listen to it.

I was having a coaching session with a client many years ago who's really bright and diligent. She had moved into a client-facing role which required her to pitch for new business and to present to big groups. As long as I'd been coaching her, she wasn't quite hitting her stride. The feedback from the business wasn't great despite her putting 100% effort into it and doing everything they asked of her, and this was being reflected in her bonus. She really felt under the microscope and the pressure was getting to her. Interestingly, during this time she volunteered to help out a colleague and do a piece of work that required huge attention to detail, structure and a high level of technical competence. My client nailed it without having to break a sweat, something other people wouldn't have had a clue how to do. She did it effortlessly and got great feedback from the business. I suggested that although it was admirable that she was trying the client-facing stuff and was showing such determination to succeed, it was actually the technical side where her superpowers lay. And that's where she would shine if she chose to make a move. Which I'm delighted to say she has.

> *"The whole secret of a successful life is to find out what is one's destiny to do, and then do it."*
> **HENRY FORD, INDUSTRIALIST AND BUSINESS MAGNATE**

ACTION/CONSIDERATION

Are there any parts of your life where you feel you're not honouring your True Nature? Or where you feel out of place?

What's the first step you can take to change this?

Do you compare your life to others? How does this affect you?

What are you going to do about it?

What do you know you're good at? What have you been told you're good at?

What comes naturally and easily to you? What environments or situations do you thrive in?

Here are some ideas to get you going:

Good with your hands, practical, working out problems, fixing things, bringing people together, communicating, managing or leading others, getting others to do things, managing projects, coming over well on the phone, being passionate about a cause, in front of people, behind a screen, in the background, on stage, performing, talking to people, talking to strangers, handling conflict, communicating ideas, analysing data, writing, being kind and compassionate, creating something from nothing, helping people, using your initiative, working with numbers, good at seeing the big picture, high attention to detail.

PEARL 5

Define YOUR version of success

> *"Try not to become a man of success, but rather try to become a man of value."*
> **ALBERT EINSTEIN, THEORETICAL PHYSICIST**

You can change the words above to read **person or woman** but I think we both know what Albert was getting at.

While we're on the subject of honouring your True Nature and carving out your own way of doing things, I wanted to share a little Pearl that I've probably only embraced myself in later life. But I think it might help you gain a stronger inner sense of who you are and what you stand for. And it's this.

You don't need to be a slave to society's or the media's definition of *"success"*.

It's an extremely subjective word and it's very easy for you to fall into the trap of defining your success – or otherwise – by what others think, rather than by what *you* think.

You can see success in so many different ways and from so many perspectives. One of my clients is head of a business development team. She was talking to one of her sales directors about what success meant for some of their accounts. And what success meant for this particular sales director. Success was not constantly trying to bash down a door that didn't want to open. Success was actually walking away and saying "No" to overly demanding or unresponsive clients. Success meant being in a different situation in six months time rather than still trying to convert the same old potential clients that clearly weren't interested. Different perspective. Different definition of success.

Actionable advice

There's huge pressure from our culture, society and media to live life in a certain way. To conform to certain ways of being and achieving certain things which define you as "successful". Says who? So you might see a smartly dressed guy driving a very expensive car and wearing a very expensive watch. You might assume he's been "successful" to be able to afford those toys. But what if I told you he never visits his elderly parents who've both got dementia because he can't face the emotional discomfort of it all. And he couldn't face going to his son's graduation because he'd bump into his ex-wife which would be awkward. Is that successful?

Now, this doesn't mean that having money is a bad thing. God no. I just want you to decide what success looks like *for you* rather than feeling you have to conform to society's version. Which, let's face it, can be pretty shallow.

ACTION/CONSIDERATION

What does success look like for you? Are there any aspects of your life where you're chasing a vision of success that isn't your own?

Are you conforming to what you think success should be according to your peer group or social media's definition?

What might happen if you stopped and redirected your energy and intention?

PEARL 6

....

Be conscious of your programming

> *They fuck you up, your mum and dad.*
> *They may not mean to, but they do.*
> *They fill you with the faults they had*
> *And add some extra, just for you.*
>
> **PHILIP LARKIN, ENGLISH POET, NOVELIST AND**
> **LIBRARIAN, FROM THIS BE THE VERSE**

So the general idea, as far as I understand it, is to operate from your True Nature wherever possible and life will flow more easily. But that's a lot easier said than done. Why? Because most of us are operating from what I call our *"acquired personality"* and that's where it can all go tits up.

Let me explain what I mean by that.

Bless you, you exploded on to this planet as we all did, as a messy screaming ball of flesh. I want you to imagine that

30

little ball of loveliness as a bright, shiny new computer. A computer that's super-powerful but totally useless until it's got some software installed. It has some in-built mechanisms like your unique blueprint and various human capacities. But the rest needs downloading. So, for about the first seven years of your precious life, you downloaded everything that you observed and heard. You sponged it all up. The good stuff and an awful lot of crap. You watched your parents. How they interacted with the world and with each other. What their thoughts were about money, achievement and success, relationships, sex, religion, politics, whether the glass is half full or half empty, whether the world is out to get you or whether it's a nice place. All of it. You just sucked it all up.

With no filters whatsoever.

And according to scientists delving into this stuff,* over 60 per cent of our daily thoughts and beliefs are negative, disempowering, self-sabotaging and limiting.

Holy fuck.

So when I talk about your acquired personality, what this means is that only a small percentage of your current thoughts are actually coming from your adult conscious mind. Most of them are coming from your subconscious and let me tell you, for the most part, they're not doing you any favours. A lot of our current behaviours are based on past conditioning and old patterns. The negative images, fears and beliefs which keep us stuck in the past. So it's no wonder you might not be living the life you want to live. You want the man or woman of your dreams to waltz into your life and sweep you off your feet? Who wouldn't? But if somewhere buried in your brain there's a programme running called "Mac OS: 12.6.78 I don't deserve to be loved" or "I'm not worthy" or a piece of software that sneaked in called "I'm afraid of being hurt again" it's going to be tough.

Even if your family was highly nurturing and empowering and didn't impose too many limitations or points of view on you, you'll still have encountered tough times and traumatic or difficult experiences growing up. We all have. And the science is telling us** that these unprocessed emotions and traumas get stored in your body energetically. They become part of you and define the way you think and behave.

Actionable advice

OK – so what can we do about it?

Part of you becoming your true self is understanding the fears and limiting beliefs that hold you back from stepping into who you really are. Fear comes in all types of shapes and sizes. Rejection, loss, separation, failure, letting others down. The list goes on and on. And all have knock-on effects on how you behave today.

Fear won't just go away but the first step is to be honest enough to admit it. And that honesty starts within you. Being able to write or speak about what you feel, what you need and what's happened to you is important. But ideally a private practice with someone you trust. Be careful who you share with.

You won't always be 100% responsible for the situation you find yourself in, but you can be damn sure you'll have had *some* role to play in it. What I know is that it's much easier to shift the responsibility on to the external world, to blame external events or others for where we're at. Look at your patterns. If you're finding yourself in the same situation again and again – relationships are a classic for this – you *have* to ask yourself, "what part did *I* play in creating this situation?" And we're very clever. We'll make up all kinds of stories to convince ourselves it's the external world at play. I've heard: "There aren't any good men/women out there. That's why I haven't been successful at dating." This might sound tough but I tend to disagree. Almost everything starts with you. Is it your limiting or negative beliefs about yourself? Is it your fears? Your controlling behaviours? What you're projecting to the outside world?

So I suggest you start to get a better understanding of why you behave the way you do. What *are* the beliefs that drive you? By taking a close look at your current behaviours and beliefs, you can consciously decide to make different choices and adopt new behaviours. You'll create new neural pathways and thought patterns which will make you behave differently.

I was talking to a client the other day who said to me that he's always looking for something to go wrong. Always looking for problems. I suggested he change his mindset to start expecting miracles instead. If he *can* change his habitual thought patterns, I just know his life will change for the better. It's already starting to change and I can't wait to see what happens when he applies himself and *really* kicks that limiting belief into touch.

> *"If you do not expect the unexpected, you will not find it."*
> **HERACLITUS, ANCIENT PHILOSOPHER**

God bless 'em, most parents are very well meaning. But no one gets a handbook. If you've grown up with parents who were risk-averse and cautious or fearful about lack of money, that's going to have some impact on you. And you could go one way or the other. Follow their footsteps *or* decide to think completely differently. Even beliefs and behaviours like "don't make a fuss", "don't say what you really think" can have detrimental consequences later on in your life. Just know you have an opportunity to do something about it. If you choose to.

Talking therapy, specific courses or coaching, or communicating directly with the subconscious through hypnotherapy will shine a light on your habitual patterns. Somatic practices, breathwork or bodywork like EFT (Emotional Freedom Technique, commonly known as tapping) is proving very effective in bringing up emotional stuff that's buried so it can be worked on and released.

ACTION/CONSIDERATION

*Which areas of your life are not working
as well as you'd like?*

*Which bits of your programming are
holding you back?*

*What stories are you telling yourself about the
outside world in order to distract you from
your limiting beliefs?*

PEARL 7

Understand the importance of balancing your masculine and feminine energy

> *"There's a balance here of yin and yang, a dance between aggression and gentleness that creates real strength in any warrior. Attack, and fall back. Thrust and parry. It's beautiful, really."*
> *Mulan thrust her sword forward and then skipped back.*
> *"A balance of yin and yang," she repeated. "I don't have to turn myself into a man to fight or rule. And I don't have to be a docile woman like my ministers expect me to be. I can be gentle and strong as circumstances require."*
> **LIVIA BLACKBURNE, AUTHOR**

The Taoists believed that there are two complementary forces that make up all aspects of life. And the way they interplay between each other is a description of the actual process of the universe and everything in it. Yin and Yang. You may have seen the symbol? The two are shown as the light and dark halves of a circle. And we all know that the masculine and feminine clearly have different attributes and different strengths. This little Pearl of Wisdom is about understanding and appreciating feminine energy and being more aware of the internal balance between your masculine and feminine. It's also about realising that you don't have to turn yourself into a man to play in a man's world.

Over the years, both personally and professionally, I've come across women of all ages who are energetically out of balance and deeply rooted in their masculine energy. They feel the need to fight and be competitive, to control, to be feared and, at worst, to be aggressive, bullying and rude. I call her the Alpha Female and I used to come across a few of them in the City. They'd often hang out in the HR department of an investment bank and some of them were brutal. These women had clearly sucked up the belief that in order to get on in a man's world, they had to behave in this way. But why turn yourself into an over-expressed Alpha Male when as a woman you've been given an entirely different set of natural superpowers, skills and abilities? Which, by the way, are supremely effective. Unfortunately, there's still a view in our society which I'm sorry to say can sometimes be perpetuated by women themselves, that the feminine is weak and the masculine is strong. Which I think is misguided.

> *"Trying to be a man is a waste of a woman."*
> **COCO CHANEL, FRENCH FASHION DESIGNER AND BUSINESSWOMAN**

Actionable advice

Feminine energy enables more ready access to the receptive qualities of intuition, listening and nurturing. The feminine style tends to be more collaborative and empathetic and recognises the need to harness different skills and backgrounds to bring diversity to a situation.

Intuition is deeply rooted in the feminine. We're all born with this innate ability to instinctively "know" something. But most people don't trust their intuition, probably because we haven't quite sussed what it is and where it comes from. I see intuition as being a bit like an internal satnav, linked to all the possible information that's available. Some of the most successful creatives and innovators, tech billionaires and heads of organisations, artists, writers and musicians rely on their intuition to tell them what to write, create and paint. So my message to you is that if your intuition is guiding you to something, don't fight it. Don't ignore it because you can't rationalise it.

I used to work with a woman who was very rooted in her masculine, very much defined by the close relationship she had with her father. She saw being "emotional" and "feminine" as weak, I think partly because she didn't understand the power of the feminine. Emotions are barometers of how you're doing. They come up to be recognised and processed. Ignore them at your peril. To recognise emotions in others and to be comfortable with the vulnerability of expressing your own is a fundamental part of the feminine and shouldn't be denied. Women also have naturally heightened sensitivity and can pick up on sensory signals. On the whole, we tend to be better than those with more masculine energy at reading facial expressions and more subtle emotional non-verbal cues. Your ability to "read a room" is extremely important. Especially at work.

The other problem with being too rooted in your masculine energy as a woman has to do with something called "polarity". Polarity is the spark or magnetic pull that attracts one person to another and creates that chemical passion. Where there's intimacy and a sexual attraction, polarity exists. It happens between the two opposing energies of the yin and the yang. Now just to be clear here, when I'm talking about *masculine* and *feminine*, I'm *not* talking about male and female. Whether you identify as male, female or gender neutral, we all have *both* masculine and feminine energies within us. In order for the chemistry to work well, one partner needs to provide more of the masculine polarity and one more of the feminine.

So what happens when this is out of balance?

Remember the Alpha Female? Now imagine that same woman wants to attract a strong, masculine man into her life. If she's more rooted in her masculine, there's a chance she'll end up attracting men who are more in their feminine. They'll be attracted by her "strength". She may end up making most of the decisions, controlling the show, being in charge. Which is fine if that's what you want. But a lot of women, if they're really honest, don't actually want that. That's precisely what happened to the woman I worked with. She ended up getting very frustrated as the man she married wouldn't take the lead or make decisions which drove her bats.

As a heterosexual woman or as someone with more feminine energy, the question you need to answer *truthfully* is "how do you want to feel with your masculine partner?" If your answer is anything along the lines of safe, secure, protected, cared for, looked after, then you need to be mindful of how *you're* showing up. And this doesn't mean you can't look after yourself. You can still be a woman with strong boundaries and strong opinions, who's independent, self-sufficient, ambitious and challenging. But, if you take it too far and are too rooted in your masculine, you could run into problems. A lot of men want strong women with their own mind, opinions and views but *they don't want to compete for who's got the biggest balls.*

> *"Femininity is a lot of power. It's allure. And the moment you start competing directly with a man, it's not that fun."*
> **CAROLINA HERRERA, FASHION DESIGNER**

Worst-case scenario, you find yourself parenting your masculine partner, telling them what to do and taking the lead most of the time. This can result in a loss of trust and respect for their abilities. They become emasculated. You end up frustrated and that is not an ideal recipe for a romantic partnership or a great sex life.

Please realise you don't have to let your masculine side dominate or overcompensate to operate or be "successful" in a left-brain masculine workplace. If you're showing up too much in your masculine, you may be compromising some of these God-given feminine superpowers. And if you don't like the way you have "to be" to get on at work – if being aggressive and competitive is the only way you can survive – maybe the culture of your organisation is actually at odds with your authentic True Nature?

ACTION/CONSIDERATION

Are you playing fully to your strengths as a woman or are you employing too many masculine traits to achieve and "succeed"?

Do you trust your intuition?

How comfortable are you with vulnerability and showing emotion?

Is the nature of your work forcing you into being competitive rather than collaborative?

If you're in a relationship, how does the balance of masculine and feminine work?

What could you do to come more into balance?

PEARL 8

Reconnect with your feminine self

> *"The reason why a lot of women are struggling to be in their feminine vibe/energy is because they refuse, knowingly or unknowingly, to tap into their sensuality, which is the grace that's always been available to them from birth."*
> **LEBO GRAND, AUTHOR, SENSUAL LIFESTYLE**

Stepping into the feminine aspect of yourself can be an act of supreme strength. For a lot of women this will feel counterintuitive and tough. When I was doing the research for this book, I asked one of my female clients what would be the most useful bit of wisdom she could use right now. Her reply slightly surprised me at the time but I've seen it more and more since. She said she felt very disconnected from her body and her feminine cycle.

Many women spend too much time in their heads. And this isn't helpful because, like my client, they've lost the relationship and connection with their bodies. Consider how refreshing it would be not to overthink, overanalyse and overrationalise your decisions. Truly stepping into the feminine is about *embodiment*. And the clue, my lovely, is in the word. *It happens in the body*. It's about getting back to *feeling*.

Actionable advice

Embodiment is about starting to experience the feelings of being a feminine woman. And it's not just about putting on a pretty dress and getting your nails painted. As lovely as that is, what I'm talking about here is reclaiming the relationship you have with your physical body. The connection back to your basic primeval feminine happens in your body, not your head. Developing a conscious relationship with your body is key to accepting yourself more easily and thriving in life. The sad thing is there are so many women who just don't like, let alone love, their bodies. Shame, guilt and fear are just some of the emotions that come up when women talk about their bodies. But there are some rituals and exercises that can help you connect back to your sensuality and femininity if this feels like something you'd like to have a go at.

Sensuality is about reconnecting to your five senses. Bringing your sensory capacity to life. It's about fully feeling the taste of a gorgeous glass of wine or a mouthful of a wonderful meal. It's about feeling the sensations in your body when you exercise, luxuriating in a massage or a hot, bubbly bath or fully feeling your orgasm. Doing more activity that reconnects you to your body is a great start. Anything that requires you to get out of your head and into your body. Cooking, pottery, painting, yoga, breathwork, Pilates, boxing, t'ai chi, gardening, crafting, dance. Whatever it is. Do it for the pure enjoyment of using your body, feeling how it feels. The sensation of the soil on your hands as you dig into the earth. The feeling of the butter and the flour as you use your fingers to crumble the mixture. The feeling of the paintbrush as an extension of your arm. The clay on your hands. You can do so much of this at home. Put some music on and dance round the kitchen. Move your body. Could you sign up for a course that gets you out of your head and into your body? Belly dancing is becoming really popular because it's not only great exercise, but it reconnects women to their very feminine essence. It teaches them how to move in a way that feels deeply authentic and a teensy bit sexy.

As well as doing these sorts of "organised" activities, there are other ways you can work on reconnecting with your body. When you operate much of your life from the neck upwards, the connection and depth you feel with your lower body suffers. So the idea here is to reconnect with the lower part of your body. Your hips, your belly, your pelvis, your sacrum. You need to start inhabiting that part of your body more. Remember, we're all made of energy. The energy in that lower part of your body might need a wake-up call.

So ideally with some music on and ideally on your own, get on all fours and start to rotate and move your hips and your lower back. If you do yoga, the cat-and-cow stretch where you arch your back and then dip your back is a good place to start. There's no right or wrong way to do this. The important thing is to spend some time moving your hips and your bum in a rhythmic way. Sway and move to the music. Rotate your lower body. Bring in your arms, release your shoulders. Just move in a sensual connected way. There's no one watching. Just get a little sexy with it. Breathe deeply into your belly. Move with the music. Touch your body if that feels good. Just go with the flow. Get into your feminine flow. *

One of my female clients made me laugh the other day. But what she was talking about was important. So, she had builders in refitting the whole of her downstairs. Major stress. She's a CFO and was at the point in the year where she had to present all her financial forecasts to her board. Pretty stressful. And she's got two young kids. Perfect storm.

She told me, "I really lost my shit at the weekend."
"Fair enough," I said.

Then her husband, very tactfully, said that he'd been listening to a podcast about a female CEO who organises her monthly diary around her menstrual cycle. Suddenly, my client, who wears a coil, so doesn't have periods, had a *massive* aha moment.

"So *that's* why I felt so stressed and emotional."
Ta-dah.

Women have not only lost their connection to their physical bodies, they've lost the relationship they have with their monthly cycle. The fundamental essence of womanhood.

Which is bloody complex, by the way.

> *"Bright girls are bold and confident. They're not ashamed or scared of their period or their body."*
> **DEMI SPACCAVENTO, AUTHOR AND SPEAKER**

During each month, your body goes through huge hormonal fluctuations. And those phases make you feel different. At certain times of the month, you might feel like a warrioress. At other times, you might feel like killing someone. And sometimes, you might feel like you can't get your gorgeous arse out of bed. And you know what? It might just be worthwhile knowing where you're at in the month. Just so you can plan a bit more. Even if you just *realise* what's causing you to feel the way you do, *that's* at least a comfort. My client thought she was losing the plot until she realised why she reacted the way she did.

And of course there's an app just waiting to help you. You may have come across "cycle syncing". Basically, it's about organising your life round your cycle so you optimise your mood, performance, sleep, nutrition and metabolism. Which could be a game changer? Just be careful about which app you choose and do your research.

ACTION/CONSIDERATION

How do you feel about your body?

What could you do to get more in touch with your body on a regular basis?

Do you feel you want to move more? How could you create your own embodiment practice?

How do you feel about monitoring your cycle?

Would it be useful to know where you are at any point in the month?

PEARL 9

·······················

Learn to receive

> *"Ask for help. Not because you are weak. But because you want to remain strong."*
> **LES BROWN, POLITICIAN AND MOTIVATIONAL SPEAKER**

Another area where a lot of us really struggle to embrace a fundamental part of our feminine is the ability to receive. And a classic example of this is our absolute resistance to ask for help. We think we need to do everything ourselves. Be independent. Be capable. Be Superwoman. Somehow, at some point, many of us sucked up the belief that not being able to do everything was "weak".

Time to change the record, my lovelies.

Actionable advice

OK, for women everywhere, we have to dispel the myth that we "don't need anything". We need to face into the fact that we, like everyone else on this planet, are imperfect. We struggle. We need help. And even in our intimate relationships, some of us are unable to be vulnerable and open up to being hurt and saying what we really need. There are a number of damaging beliefs we've taken on board about asking for help. "They'll think I'm high maintenance", "Someone will use it against me in the future", "I can't show that I'm not capable of doing everything". Read this quote from Brené Brown. And once you've read it, read it again.

> *"Until we can receive with an open heart, we are never really giving with an open heart. When we attach judgment to receiving help, we knowingly or unknowingly attach judgment to giving help."*
> **BRENÉ BROWN,**
> **PROFESSOR, RESEARCHER AND AUTHOR**

And this is a problem. Why are you trying to be Superwoman? And then be constantly knackered? It just doesn't make sense. If you train your partner and children to sit there while you do *everything*, that becomes the expectation. You've just made a wonderful rod for your own back.

I've struggled with this my whole life. Guilty as charged, m'lud. My instant reaction whenever anybody asked me if I wanted help was, "No thanks, I'm fine." It was my default response and I didn't even think about the consequences of refusing help. Shit, I now have to lug this fucking heavy suitcase up three flights of stairs. Duh. How smart *is* that really? Nowadays if someone asks me if I need help, I'm a lot more likely to say something like, "You know what, that would be really fab, thank you." A strapping young railway employee offered to carry my suitcase down the station steps the other day. I just managed to stop myself saying, "No thanks, I'm fine." Instead, I gave him a big smile (the special one I use for strapping young railway employees), thanked him and handed him my suitcase.

Asking for help isn't a sign of weakness. Let your masculine partner lead, let them look after you, let them help you. Let go of trying to control everything. Learn to kick back sometimes. Allow others to do some housework or make you a cup of tea. They'll respect you far more if you start putting some boundaries in place. It takes self-awareness and courage to admit that either you can't do everything or actually that you *don't want to* and that you could use some help. Just allow yourself to be helped. Try it. I used to have a male friend round for the occasional supper. I'd do the prep. I'd serve up. I'd clear up. I'd fill the dishwasher. He'd just sit at the kitchen table. Until I asked him to peel the potatoes for the roasts and clear up the plates from the table. He gladly obliged and got stuck in. I realised he was actually quite happy to help. I'd just made him lazy by doing everything myself and not asking. According to the Taoist definition, the masculine energy is focused, action orientated, full of direction and purpose. It's about pushing forward, controlling, giving, leading and taking care of stuff. So why not use it? I suspect the guy who helped me with my suitcase probably got something out of it, felt good about himself helping an old girl with her case! Win-win, I say.

Compliments are another classic example of women refusing to receive. Pay a woman a compliment and many of us throw it right back. "Nice dress"…"Oh God, this old thing, I've had it for years, picked it up at a charity shop." "Your hair looks nice"… "Oh really. It needs washing/cutting/colouring." "I *love* your handbag"… "Oh, it's a fake."

FFS, just *receive* it graciously.

> *"Always take a compliment, Caroline. Always take it for the way it was intended. You girls are always so quick to twist what others say. Simply say thank you and move on."*
> **ALICE CLAYTON, AUTHOR, WALLBANGER**

Let me give you my take on receiving a compliment. You've heard of basking sharks? Now why do you think they're called basking sharks? Because they lie on the surface of the water and soak up the sun's rays. When you receive a compliment, I want you to *bask* in it. Soak it up. Allow it to seep into your very fabric. Enjoy it and acknowledge it. Both to yourself and to the person who gave it to you. I just want you to say two words, simple as that. *"Thank you."* End of. Take a compliment like a shark! If you negate it, you're throwing it back in the face of the person who gave it to you. A compliment is their opinion. You can't tell them their opinion is wrong!

> *"A compliment is verbal sunshine."*
> **ROBERT ORBEN, COMEDY WRITER**

There's so much emphasis nowadays on the virtue of giving, but there's a balance to be had. I'm a fan of "give and it shall be given unto you". But, it's important to be able to receive too. And that could be anything – from gifts to compliments, love or help.

ACTION/CONSIDERATION

What's your core belief about asking for help?

In which parts of your life could you ask for help more often?

Is there anyone you need to re-educate to help you more?

How do you generally take a compliment?

How do you feel about saying thank you and basking?

PEARL 10

Understand what
Good Selfish is all about

> "You don't have to be overwhelmed to
> begin meeting your needs."
> **KOBE CAMPBELL, MENTAL HEALTH
> COUNSELLOR, AUTHOR AND SPEAKER**

"Should an emergency situation occur, put your own oxygen mask on first, before attempting to help those around you." You'll hear words like these or something similar, when you board any aircraft around the world. You might be thinking this sounds selfish and counterintuitive, but it's based on good old-fashioned common sense. You simply can't be of use to anyone else unless you're what I call "fully resourced" yourself. How can you expect to be on top form for others if you're not meeting your needs? And this isn't about constantly putting your needs *above* others'. It's about honouring your own needs rather than denying them. Put your own mask on first, then you can be of service to others.

> *"Taking care of yourself is the most powerful
> way of taking care of others."*
> **BRYANT MCGILL, HUMAN-POTENTIAL
> THOUGHT LEADER, AUTHOR, SPEAKER**

Actionable advice

There may be occasions when it's totally appropriate to put someone else's needs above your own. But, if you have a tendency to *consistently* say No when you mean Yes and Yes when you mean No in order to please others, it's time to look at what's going on. Because this is a path to misery. And sometimes it's not even about pleasing others. It's about keeping the peace with your harsh inner critic. It's about keeping your Perfectionist happy. 'Needs' can be physical. Enough sleep, proper nutrition, hydration, exercise, the need to pee, a break from the computer, a break from the news/social media, some fresh air. Needs can be emotional. Someone to talk to, time alone, space to reflect and process, time with friends/family. Needs can be spiritual. Time to connect with a higher power, pray, meditate, time to nourish your soul. You'll know what you need. Your body will certainly tell you if you listen to it. And it will *absolutely* tell you if you constantly ignore it. Panic attacks are a classic example of this. That's your body sending out a distress signal.

Now you know this stuff in theory, but can you honestly say you're attending to your needs on a regular basis? When I ask people why they ignore their needs, they say things like "people will think I'm being a pain or high maintenance or self-centred". Believing you're unworthy can be another reason. If you recognise this, it's time for you to build some new habits. If you feel the answer is Yes, as hard as it may be, you must *say* Yes instead of No. If you feel the answer is No – say it. Or say something that means No. Every time you negate your real feelings, you chip away at your self-worth and self-esteem.

A "look after number one" attitude isn't meant to turn you into a self-centred narcissist. And neither is it about over-exaggerating your needs so you have no resilience and become incapable of doing the most basic tasks. This is about resourcing yourself so you *can* show up strongly for others. You can do a lot of good in the world if you're in a healthy place yourself. If nothing else, you're sending a message to yourself that you're worthy. Worthy of other people's time, worthy of being cared for and nurtured. Practising *maitri*. For yourself. We all know what Bad Selfish looks like. Good Selfish is very different.

When I was managing the care for my mum and dad, the district nurse took me aside on one of her visits. She asked me how *I* was coping. I burst into tears. Embarrassing? Yes, but absolutely necessary. I was conscious of taking care of my physical needs well enough but possibly neglecting my emotional ones. I didn't want to burden friends and family with discussing my parents' decline. And a lot of us *don't* open up precisely because we think we *might* just burst into tears or get overly emotional. So what? If you don't get emotional about something very upsetting, that's pretty sad. Close friends and family *should* be there to support you. And if you don't feel they are, maybe that's another conversation you need to have? So don't be afraid to get your emotional needs met by opening up and telling the right people how things really are. Honour your feelings rather than ignoring them. Anything you can do to replenish yourself and be as resourced as you can be, do it.

ACTION/CONSIDERATION

Is there a part of your life where you're not meeting your needs?

Are there occasions where you're consistently putting others' needs above your own to your own detriment?

PEARL 11

Stop people pleasing

> *"There's something very addictive about people pleasing. It's a thought pattern and a habit that feels really, really good until it becomes desperate."*
>
> **ANNE HATHAWAY, ACTRESS**

"People pleasing" is so common you might not even realise you're doing it. The problem is that if it gets out of hand you start fixating so much on what others want, you disconnect from your own needs. Focusing on others can become the only way you feel valued and worthy. And we really don't want you falling into that trap.

A bit like the Imposter and the Perfectionist, the People Pleaser is nothing more than fear in disguise. It just wants love and approval. But it'll throw you under the bus to get it. And it can show up at any time. Could be from your boss, your partner or often from your *family*. Yes, that old pigeon. And that's where much of this comes from. The thing about family is *all* that history you've built up over the years. The way they treat you or speak to you, has been the same since you were a kid. And no-one questions it. Family dynamics are just classic for people pleasing and poor boundaries. Ringing any bells? With your parents or siblings? Do you ever slip back into childhood patterns?

I've got friends with older siblings. They're all in their fifties and sixties now but they're still playing out the same old bullshit childhood patterns. My friend, who has an older brother, still gets treated like the baby. But the funny thing is, she still plays along with it. She still doesn't call out his appalling temper tantrums. She still doesn't want to offend him or make him lose his shit. She still doesn't want to "upset the apple cart". So he gets away with behaving like an absolute arse. Like he's always done. Nothing's changed since they were kids. They've just got more grey hair.

The other place your People Pleaser might show up is at work. Some people at work can take the piss. Even if they don't mean to. If you keep saying Yes, then you're giving them permission to keep asking for more of your precious time and energy. And then, just to add insult to injury, your inner critic poles up and beats you up. "Why the fuck did you agree to do that?" So you end up in a socking great people-pleasing cycle of misery. So let's not go there.

> *"All the mistakes I ever made were when I wanted to say 'No' and I said 'Yes'."*
> **MOSS HART, PLAYWRIGHT AND**
> **THEATRE DIRECTOR**

Your worthiness is not dependent on other people's approval. However, your happiness is *highly* dependent on how strong your boundaries are in your personal relationships. Clearly communicating your boundaries is one of the keys to your personal freedom and one of the ways you'll stop yourself becoming a serial people pleaser.

Actionable advice

You've got to have boundaries in your life to distinguish what's your responsibility and what isn't. What will you tolerate? What won't you tolerate? What is and isn't acceptable to you?

> *"Boundaries protect the things that are of value to you. They keep you in alignment with what you have decided you want in life. That means the key to good boundaries is knowing what you want."*
> **ADELYN BIRCH, AUTHOR**

Sounds easy in theory, doesn't it? But we all know how hard it actually is. Most of us are afraid to even *set* boundaries because we're worried about the consequences.

> *"The inability to set appropriate boundaries at appropriate times with the appropriate people can be very destructive."*
> **DR HENRY CLOUD AND DR JOHN TOWNSEND, CO-AUTHORS, BOUNDARIES: WHEN TO SAY YES AND WHEN TO SAY NO**

Our fear of offending, annoying and pissing people off can turn us into irrational human beings. Many people are obsessed about being "nice" which is admirable, but not consistently to your own detriment. And setting boundaries doesn't mean you're not being nice. You're just looking after yourself. It's also about reframing those beliefs you sucked up as a child about not being worthy, having to be nice to everyone and hating to let people down. But if you're able to have a grown-up, rational conversation about your needs and wants, what you're prepared to put up with and what you're not, life will be a whole load more enjoyable.

And you'll come across certain types of people in life who'll really test your boundaries. People who are controlling will see a boundary as a challenge. Controlling people often don't take responsibility for their own lives, so they like to try and control others'. There are certain individuals who'll take you for granted. And be aware of those family members who know which buttons to press. If they hit your guilt button, are you just going to roll over and do whatever they want? So be more mindful of those individuals where you need to bring more awareness and strength to your boundaries.

The first stage in boundary setting is to understand what you want. What will you put up with? What can't you put up with? Everyone's tolerances are different. You might be happy to work til 7 or 8pm every night because you know it's for a short time. You're going to get a big fat bonus at the end of the quarter or the year. And that might be OK with you. Or you may be happy with it now but you know you can't sustain it and neither do you want to. *OR* this doesn't feel good on any level, and you think they're taking advantage of you.

The key to this is about going inside and being really honest about how you *feel* about a situation. Most people's default is to override the feeling with an automatic "Oh it's fine" when actually it's not. You feel resentment. You're angry. So name it. Mostly, you know when someone has breached one of your boundaries. When someone says or does something that doesn't feel good to you. Because that's precisely the point. It shows up in your body as a feeling. You'll have an emotional response or maybe a stronger emotional reaction that makes you angry. Sometimes a knotty feeling in the pit of your stomach. Or a tightening in your chest. You know it doesn't feel good but you might not know how to deal with it.

> *"When you say 'Yes' to others, make sure you're not saying 'No' to yourself."*
> **PAULO COELHO, AUTHOR**

It's really the second part about expressing those feelings that most people find challenging.

So if you know you struggle with this, start practising saying No in a way that feels OK to you. Or think about the best way to explain to your partner that some aspect of their behaviour is making you feel like you're being taken for granted. It might be that you need more help with the domestics or childcare. It might be turning down an evening out with friends, when you're knackered but you feel obliged or guilty. What do you really want to say? Something like, "I actually need to go home and just zap out", "I'd rather not, I need to rest...", "I really need to stay put this evening", "I've got a whole bunch of things I really need to get done tonight, I'll come with you another time".

Or at work, "If I do that then I won't have time to finish this... which would you prefer me to do?", "What's your deadline?" (always ask this question), "I'm going to struggle to get that done today. I've got time on Friday, does that work?" Clearly you want to show you are willing with someone like your boss but without causing yourself a problem. Constantly working late because you can't say No is unsustainable. Sometimes getting your boss to prioritise your time is a good strategy. Particularly if you work for several people. Make it clear you can do one or the other but *not both*.

I was playing tennis with an old friend the other day. We've known each other for years and she was saying how difficult she used to find it to say No. She reminded me of a phrase that I'd suggested she use all those years ago and how helpful it had been in keeping her boundaries firm. *"That doesn't work for me."* She said she used to pre-fix it with "sorry" but she's dropped the "sorry" now. Really no need to apologise. Now that worked for her; it might not work for you. It's very subjective and some phrases and words work for some people and not others.

Choosing *how* you're going to say what you want to say is key. Your boundaries need to be communicated in a way that's assertive and authentic. Assertive means respect for self and respect for others. It's pleasant but it's firm. It's about finding the words that work best for you to express how you feel about what's happened or what's happening on a regular basis. I suggest you play around with what you want to say out loud in a rational, non-emotional way. If someone has breached one of your boundaries and it causes an emotional reaction, it's a good idea to wait to discuss it until the emotional fallout has subsided. You need to be able to communicate in a grounded and strong way without the emotion clouding the picture.

If someone isn't hearing you or taking you seriously, you'll need to strengthen your language or your tone of voice. The other thing you can do which is super useful is to use a pause after you say something. It's like you're saying "have you got that?" Imagine someone you know who can take you for granted sometimes, asks you a favour, assuming you'll say Yes. *"That's not going to work for me"* or *"I'm not going to be able to do that"* (pause). The pause will also stop you *justifying* your reason. You don't have to give a reason. Just like you don't need to apologise.

If you're with someone who isn't actually taking the piss and you want to be accommodating but just can't do what they want – just say you can't do it but then follow it up with a question to explore alternatives. "What other options are available? What other times do you have? What else might work for you?"

Have you ever volunteered to do something that deep down you didn't want to do? Was it about earning validation or recognition? And I know sometimes it can be really well meaning. Because you felt strongly about something and no-one else was bothering to step up? Sitting on a school committee? Organising something in the community? Volunteering to take on extra stuff at work? Captaining a sports team? Try negotiating to do *some* of it, just not *all* of it. Or, just keep your bloody mouth shut. And tell yourself you're not going to offer because deep down you really just don't want to do it. You're choosing not to. *And that's perfectly OK.* You have to start behaving differently, saying things a little differently.

And when you do have the courage to start behaving differently, you'll find others will react differently. If you're not available, accessible, willing to say yes, offering to help, pleasing, you'll start to see a different kind of response in others. I've seen a number of cases where this has been *forced* on people. Something happens in their lives that actually forces them to say No. Looking after elderly parents means you physically don't have time and energy to do something else. So much work you're drowning and on the edge of physical collapse, or having panic attacks, so you're forced to say No. It would be good for you to be able to say No before life reaches crisis point. And yes, people might be a bit pissed off to start with. But you know, it's also likely they'll stop taking you for granted. You'll get a lot more respect when you hold true to your boundaries and don't cave in. The plain truth of it is that people pleasers aren't as respected as people who've got stronger boundaries. So if you want more respect, get cracking on how you're going to say *No* in a way that feels OK to you. Just a little more often, when it feels right.

> *"Don't set yourself on fire to keep others warm."*
> **ANONYMOUS**

The other day I was talking to a really talented young woman who told me she was a people pleaser. She wasn't standing up for herself or communicating her needs. Her boss frequently rang her in the evening about work. She didn't feel like she could go out after work as she always had to be "on call". She was being held back by her boss and felt she wasn't progressing. She asked me whether I thought she should look for a new job. You know what I said to her?

> *"Wherever you go, there you are."**

You can't run away from your stuff. We've all got baggage and issues. That's the journey. By moving jobs and running away, she wasn't going to solve anything. Different people, same shit. The people pleasing will follow her wherever she goes, until she finds the courage to have the conversations she needs to have and put some boundaries in place. And don't you think it's going to be easier with people she knows rather than starting all over again? Of course, if she does repeatedly have these conversations and *still* her boss doesn't change, then yes, maybe it's time to move on. Perhaps it's her boss who needs to look at why he's behaving like he is?

ACTION/CONSIDERATION

··

In what situations do you say "Yes" when you really mean "No"?

With what kinds of people or which specific person?

How could you express your needs and boundaries differently? Say it out loud and find the words that feel right for you.

PEARL 12

....

Take off the "I'm fine" mask

> "When you constantly say things are fine, while knowing
> that you really want something more, it's called stuck."
> **MEL ROBBINS, AUTHOR, '**
> **STOP SAYING YOU'RE FINE**

We need to talk about how important it is to say how you really feel in relationships. Both at home and at work. This very British tendency to play down how we're *really* feeling can actually be pretty damaging to your mental well-being. And I just want to flag it for you so you can avoid what I call the I.F.S – The "I'm Fine Syndrome". Let me tell you about an old client of mine.

I was sitting in a meeting room in Central London, waiting to see some clients for 1:1 coaching. The first client came in and I ran through the usual intros and expectations. She was a new graduate and terribly sweet. Looked like a baby deer. All big blue eyes and long blonde hair. She started talking about her job and some of the challenges she was having.

Alarm bells immediately started to sound in my head. It was a fucking car crash. She'd been dumped well and truly in at the deep end. She knew very little about her job and pretty much nothing about the industry. One of her colleagues had gone off sick and there was no-one around to help. She was having panic attacks at the idea of picking up the phone and talking to strangers. And she wasn't really sure what she was supposed to say or do when she did get hold of people. And you know what? Once she'd finished, she looked across the table at me and with a slightly quivering lip uttered those immortal words.

"But I'm fine…"

I leant back in my chair and looked straight into those big blue eyes. "You feel shit about your job, shit about yourself as a result, you're not sleeping, you're totally stressed about turning up for work and you're having panic attacks. It doesn't sound like you're fine to me, sweetheart. It sounds like you're anything *but* fine." And with that, out came the tissues.

Actionable advice

If you recognise this tendency in yourself, the first thing you need to do when this happens is to go inside. Ask yourself, "how do I *really* feel about this?" And be brutally honest. Your own honesty needs to be louder than your parents' voices who may have brought you up to be a nice girl who doesn't "make a fuss" and "just gets on with it". You then have to tell the right people that you need help. If you don't pipe up people assume you *are* fine, that you're cracking on and everything's dandy. People are busy. You've got to be proactive. And a little bit brave. It really is OK to ask for help. We've already talked about this.

With my client, we simply needed to work out *why* it was happening. What was causing the stress and what would help her? Point one, the right people needed to understand what was going on. They were all so buried in their own work they weren't paying attention. She simply needed three things: more specific guidance and instruction, more phone training and a bit of slack on the timelines.

Never think that burying your head in the sand is a better option. The problem won't go away. In fact, it'll often get worse. You need to speak up. And you know what? Sometimes people may sense there's something wrong with you. Saying "I'm fine" can actually be unhelpful because they might think you're not being honest with them. So just be mindful, particularly if you know you have "I'm fine" tendencies. Promise me you won't go there anymore. Say something different instead. Ask the appropriate people for help if you need it.

You don't have to be a young grad to be affected by I.F.S either. It can be a default reaction at any stage of your life and in any kind of relationship. Older men and women complain about it in their marriages and intimate relationships the whole time. Women are notorious for saying "I'm fine" when steam is coming out of their ears. And they're seething. *Quietly* seething. It's somehow easier to say that rather than get into that same old, same old conversation that pisses you off so much and feels pointless. Ringing any bells? It's a classic mistake couples make but one which can chip away at a harmonious relationship if you're not careful. Make sure you take action so you don't go down this particularly slippery slope, from which sometimes there's no return.

> *"As a flower needs water and sunlight, a relationship needs good communication to grow and thrive."*
> **SASSY GODMOTHER, AUTHOR, SPEAKER AND SPIRITUAL ADVENTURER**

Hidden resentment can build if a woman feels that her partner *hasn't noticed* what she wants. She's waiting for her needs and desires to be met without actually communicating what she wants. Our partners shouldn't have to guess our needs. "He should know what I want," is what I hear from a lot of women. Well, no. I disagree. You need to tell him or her. None of us are mind readers. Yes – some people catch on more quickly than others. And they might get some of it right but in other areas you may need to make it plain. How about taking responsibility for telling your partner what you want? Communicate your needs clearly, calmly and consistently.

ACTION/CONSIDERATION

When was the last time you said "I'm fine" when you weren't?

Is there a particular area of your life (work, relationship) where you habitually say "I'm fine" when you know in your heart you're not?

Why do you say it? What do you think is going to happen if you make it clear you're not fine?

Are there any needs you have that you're not communicating to your partner? If so, why are you holding back?

How could you reopen the conversation in a different way?

PEARL 13

....

*Play and communicate for a
good sex life*

> *"Communication is the best lubrication.
> The more you talk about sex, the better it will be."*
> **EMILY MORSE, AUTHOR, SMART SEX – HOW
> TO BOOST YOUR SEX IQ AND OWN YOUR
> PLEASURE**

And while we're on the subject of communicating your
needs in a relationship, one of the most important places
that this needs to happen is in the bedroom.

Sex is the source of much pleasure. But for some, also of
much angst. The bedroom has a nasty habit of bringing out
some of our limiting beliefs, worries and insecurities. I'd say
I've lived a reasonably colourful life when it comes to sex
and the two biggest lessons I want to pass on to you are 1)
it needs to be fun and playful and 2) you need to be able to
talk about it.

Actionable advice

I see sex as adult play time. Bring your sense of humour into your bedroom. In my view, the more laughter, the better, as it reduces a lot of the angst. Yes, of course, sex can be a deeply loving and spiritual act. But sex therapists and psychologists totally agree that bringing a playful and light energy to your sex life can be a gamechanger.

Being too serious about the outcome can ruin sex. Make sure you enjoy the journey, whatever the outcome. This is where being playful comes in. Play is about enjoying the moment and not being hung up on results. Being fixated on achieving orgasm or achieving orgasm for your partner can be a route to dissatisfaction and frustration.

> *"The idea that it's one person's responsibility to give another person an orgasm can be the source of all kinds of trouble."*
> **STEPHEN SNYDER, M.D. AUTHOR, LOVE WORTH MAKING: HOW TO HAVE RIDICULOUSLY GREAT SEX IN A LONG-LASTING RELATIONSHIP**

One of the other things to remember about sex is that it's a very subjective thing. Everyone is different. Everyone responds differently to certain physical or mental stimuli. There's no one-size-fits-all approach. And that's why *communication is so important*. It's absolutely crucial that you communicate your wants, needs and preferences to your partner in the bedroom. Good communication is fundamental to a good sex life. And yet so many people just clam up and don't talk about how they're feeling. Because they think it might offend or upset. The way to manage all those insecurities and worries is to talk about what's going on for you. People will ask their partners what they want for dinner, whether they want to go out or not, whether they want to go for a walk or not. And yet, when it comes to sex, somehow we should all be mind readers. If you're tired, say so. If you're not in the mood and just want to be close and have a cuddle, say so. Don't try to please your partner, end up feeling dissatisfied and they're left wondering what's wrong with you.

Being clear about your likes and dislikes and your preferences is really important. Remember earlier on we talked about being "Good Selfish"? Be *Good Selfish* in the bedroom. Focusing on your own arousal is an important part of good sex. Don't consistently do things that you don't like and that don't turn you on. It sounds obvious, but hey. Like oral sex, for example. It's not everyone's cup of tea. If you don't get aroused by it, don't keep doing it. It will eventually sap your erotic energy. Find something else that turns you on and concentrate on that instead. *But talk about it.* And here's something else. You may have had a historical like or dislike for one thing or another with a previous partner. Don't assume that the same will be the case with *a new partner*. Be open-minded and try new things. A new partner may bring a different mindset, approach and style which could have a profoundly positive effect on you. I've experienced this and it's truly liberating.

Not only do you need to communicate *during* sex but also afterwards. And it doesn't need to be immediately afterwards. But actually saying how much you enjoyed something or how someone made you feel can have a hugely positive and validating impact on your relationship. Equally, if something didn't work so well for you then discuss it so it doesn't become the elephant in the bedroom. My partner and I will often talk about sex when we're out for a long walk. I'd encourage you to talk more freely outside the bedroom so you get used to discussing your likes, dislikes and preferences in a really non-judgemental and non-defensive way.

And if you're feeling less than great about your sex life, don't get hung up on the fairy-tale idea that everyone else out there is having great sex all the time. It isn't true, according to plenty of sex therapists and surveys. All you can do is work with your partner on making it the best it can be for you both, *according to you both*. What anyone else does is irrelevant. But just remember – keep it playful and keep talking!

ACTION/CONSIDERATION

What opportunities could you use to talk more openly with your partner about your sex life?

What could you do to bring a more playful energy into your sex life?

PEARL 14

....

Make dating work for you

> *"Dating is about finding out who you are and who others are. If you show up in a masquerade outfit, neither is going to happen."*
> **DR HENRY CLOUD, SELF-HELP AUTHOR**

You won't believe it but a good few years ago there was a real stigma about going on dating sites. Online is now the most popular place to meet a partner, husband or wife. But dating isn't for everyone. One in ten singles apparently say they feel burned out by dating. It's true that online dating can require a bit of a tough skin, but I think a lot has to do with how you approach the process and play the game.

Where else do you get the opportunity to walk into a virtual room of thousands of people, all supposedly there for the same reason? And you get to experiment and learn what works and what doesn't? It gives you a wealth of opportunity that just doesn't exist in the real world. But, there are some fundamental principles you need to apply to get the most out of the whole dating thing. You might think some of this is obvious but let's talk about it anyway.

Actionable advice

The first thing you need to look at is your ***attitude***. I dipped my toes into the world of dating apps a few years ago. Do you know what I found most striking? It seemed to me that a lot of men and women didn't actually ***want*** to be on a dating site at all. It was clearly a *"have to"* rather than a *"want to"*. And how did I come to that conclusion? Because of the number of poorly written profiles and crappy photographs. I don't know about you, but men taking selfies in the urinals is a real turn-off for me. A red flag on self-awareness. I get the whole mirror thing, but don't do it. They're rarely good. That suggested to me that very little effort had been put into the process. If you don't really want to do something or be somewhere, of course you're not going to do it well or show up fully engaged. You're not going to invest your energy into it or take it seriously. The impression I got was that frankly, a lot of men just couldn't be arsed to get decent photos done or take time to write a thoughtful profile. And I saw the same in many of the female profiles that my male friends showed me. It was disappointing.

So, first things first. Do you really ***want*** to be there? And if you *do*, show up as your full self and be prepared to invest some real time and effort. If you've paid a fee to sign up to a dating website then surely you'll want to get the most out of it? Even if you haven't, you *still* need to apply the same level of investment. Act *as if* you had paid for it. Online dating done properly is time-consuming and requires work. Your dating profile is a bit like your CV. It's your sales document. I chose apps where there was enough space for me to write a decent length profile to showcase myself properly, not just a few lines. I wanted those men looking at me to get a really good idea of who I was, what I did, how I spent my time, what I liked and what I wanted from a man and a relationship.

When you write your profile, be *so* clear and honest about who you are and what you want, that you ensure you put off the wrong people. And attract the right people. There's never been a more important occasion to be one hundred per cent authentic. Don't write what you think they want to read. Write the truth about who you are and what you want. I was talking to a friend in my singing group one day who was getting a bit jaded with the whole dating process. I was giving her some ideas on how she might change her profile. When I said about being totally authentic and putting off those guys she wouldn't click with, her eyes lit up. She's a little quirky. "You mean I can put in *don't be shocked if I sing an aria in bed*?"

"Yes," I said. "Precisely. You need to be with the kind of guy who's going to *love* you singing an aria in bed. Celebrate that part of you. Not someone who thinks you're weird. That's why you have to be totally honest about who you are. The right person will love it, the wrong person won't come anywhere near you." Great filter.

And just like your CV, it's not a time to be modest. Don't undersell yourself or your achievements, your ambitions, your desires. Be prepared to be a bit creative with your profile if that's something that you feel you could do. Stand out. Be different by being yourself. There are a lot of very boring, average and dull profiles out there.

And photographs. You've got to put yourself in the shoes of the person looking at your profile. Ideally, don't take selfies for your dating profile. Rarely do you get the best angle and shot. Get a friend to take some high-quality photos of you in different surroundings that tell people about you, what you're like, what you like doing. Take the trouble. It's also safe to say that someone might like to see your face. Make sure you get photos of your sweet self without the large Victoria Beckham face-covering specs. And if you want to put your pet on there, then get you in the picture as well. Avoid group photos where a potential partner is left guessing which one is you. You've got to ask yourself, "am I showcasing myself in the best possible way?" I can't think of a better example of "you reap what you sow" than the effort you put in to creating a really good dating profile and managing the process well. It will pay you back. It'll help avoid *some* of the pitfalls. Not all, of course. That's where your mindset and resilience are important.

So let's talk about this for a minute. The beliefs you're holding on to about yourself are going to play a big part in who you attract. There's nothing like the dating experience to bring these right up to the surface and challenge your self-esteem. All those limiting beliefs and insecurities come out to play when you get rejected, ghosted or lied to. You need resilience to cope with the ups and downs of online dating and your boundaries need to be very clear about what you expect, what you'll accept and what you won't accept. I've heard too many stories of women being treated appallingly by people they've met on dating sites – but they put up with it. And therein lies the problem.

Also – have you caught yourself saying "there's no good men/ women out there"? I know this might sound a little tough and controversial but I think that's bullshit and a blocker right from the get-go. I'd suggest you take a good look at how you're going about dating and what your mindset is. Your thinking will influence your whole experience. And yes, of course there are a lot of arseholes out there but there are also plenty of good, honest, available, decent, fun, solvent and beautiful partners waiting to find you.

> *"I know you can crave companionship and sex and love so badly that it physically hurts. But I truly believe that the only way you can find out that there's something better out there is to first believe there's something better out there. What other choice is there?"*
> **GREG BEHRENDT AND LIZ TUCCILLO, CO-AUTHORS, HE'S JUST NOT THAT INTO YOU**

The other thing that struck me was the number of people who I thought shouldn't be anywhere *near* a dating site. Like recently bereaved, recently divorced and recently separated guys on the lookout for a new relationship. For me, these are massive red flags. What are your own red flags? If you're looking for a committed relationship, the most important thing is to find someone who's *emotionally available* and who's ready to engage in a relationship. Sometimes it takes a few conversations and a potential date for someone to realise they're not ready. Best discover it early before you embark on a relationship with someone who hasn't let go of a previous relationship. You may not be looking for a committed relationship. You might just want to have some fun. But be clear on what you want. This exercise below might help clarify a few things for you.

This seemingly simple exercise will help you get absolutely clear on what it is you're looking for in your prospective partner. Think of as many qualities, attributes, preferences, personality traits and characteristics as you can and make a long list under these three columns.

The first column is self-explanatory. Anyone who doesn't meet any one of these criteria is immediately eliminated. These are absolute no-brainer, non-negotiables. Wants/doesn't want children, smoker/non-smoker, sense of humour, has own interests.

The second column lists the qualities that aren't essential but still play an important part in your choice. Likes the outdoors/walking, considerate, has opinions.

The third column are things that "would be great if"…

willing to try different holidays, likes live music. You can live without it, but life would be so much better with it.

Essential	Preferable	Desirable

Once you start dating, there are four fundamental questions that you need to be able to answer:

Is there a connection?

Do your core values align?

Is your person emotionally available and mature?

*If **you** want to settle down, how ready is that person to settle down?*

ACTION/CONSIDERATION

What is your mindset around dating?
Do you actually want to be doing it?

Where has your dating profile worked?
Where hasn't it worked? Why?

Can you bring more authenticity and
honesty to your profile? How else can you change it?

Do you need to be on a site where
you can showcase yourself better?

Are you clear on your red flags in the dating process?
What are they?

PEARL 15

....

Complain graciously but assertively

> *"The way we communicate with others and with ourselves ultimately determines the quality of our lives."*
> **ANTHONY ROBBINS, AUTHOR,**
> **COACH AND SPEAKER**

It seems to me that us Brits have never been terribly comfortable complaining. It appears to be wrapped up with the same mindset as the "I'm Fine Syndrome". Don't make a fuss. Don't make a scene. Don't make a nuisance of yourself. Stiff upper lip. Just put up with it. Sometimes I wish we could be a little more like the French. Train fares go up in France so commuters strike and protest. Classic bolshie French-ness. I just love it.

But don't wait until you get to my age to master this most basic social skill. By doing it graciously, you'll win people over. You didn't cause a scene. By the way – that's usually other people's discomfort when they tell you "don't make a fuss". It's them who feels awkward. That's their shit. Being able to complain graciously but assertively is sending a message to yourself that you're worthy. That you deserve what you've paid for. That you're important enough to be taken seriously. And heard.

So often I've seen this scenario unfold: the steak is not what I ordered and it's as tough as old boots. But I'll just sit here and eat it all up and not say a word. And not enjoy it. And then I'll pay for it. And then I'll moan about it to my friends.

WTF is *that* about?

If you don't complain, how are places ever going to learn they need to do it better? "Oh I just won't go back." "I'll give them a crappy review on Trip Advisor."

Well, that's really helpful.

Learn to complain assertively and graciously. Assertively is firm and direct but with total respect for the person you're complaining to. Sometimes I think the British hold a lot of pent-up anger because we don't complain regularly. And when we do finally get red-faced and fed up enough to say something, it can erupt into an aggressive or sarcastic reaction which isn't helpful in the slightest.

I've got to the age where I simply won't tolerate poor service. The following things will get sent back: food which isn't what I ordered. If there's a mix-up, there's a likelihood someone else has got my order and the restaurant needs to know this. Food which is not cooked how I ordered it. Food which is cold or lukewarm. Wine which is corked or oxidised. White wine which is warm. Anything which hasn't been cleaned properly, whether it's lipstick on a wine glass or a dirty hotel room. Post-Covid, most hospitality establishments are struggling with enough staff. Many haven't been trained properly, if at all. I was in a bar the other day and the young girl behind the bar didn't know how to use a corkscrew to open a bottle of wine. She should have been trained. But equally, she could have shown some initiative and asked someone to show her. Service has never been fabulous in the UK, but right now it's hit rock bottom in a lot of places.

Now, first-world-problems spoiler. This is all against a backdrop of being extremely grateful that I'm lucky enough to go to restaurants, bars and hotels. That's always something we have to remember. *But* if you're paying for something, and prices are punchy these days, there's a fair enough assumption that you should get what you ordered and how you ordered it. *And* there should be a reasonable level of service. If the food takes an hour to find its way to the table, there needs to be a conversation. Would you eat hot food that's cold at home? Probably not. Then why tolerate it when you're paying for it?

So, I'd urge you to complain if you feel you haven't got what you're paying for. It's all part of knowing what you want and not being afraid to be assertive. Remember your boundaries. If you can't complain nicely to a stranger, you're going to struggle to have tough conversations with family.

Actionable advice

Just be gracious. Be charming. Be complimentary about what's good. "The food's lovely but it's just not hot." Be polite, be pleasant, but be firm and direct. "Have you got any wine that's a bit colder?" Then pause. Smile and look them in the eye. Wait for a response. Wait for them to put it right. If they don't, then just ask for a replacement whatever it is. You're not looking for a confrontation. You're just looking for a better outcome. And stop apologising profusely when it's not your fault. "*I'm so sorry* but this steak isn't what I ordered." "*I'm afraid* this isn't what I ordered." *NO!* "*Hiya… unfortunately I asked for medium-rare and this is well done. Could you sort it out for me? Thanks so much.*" Just hand it back with a smile and wait for their response.

Treating waiting, hotel and bar staff politely is one of my core values. They're doing their job and they deserve to be treated with respect. Time and again, by being pleasant and polite, I get more. I cringe when I see people in restaurants being dismissive and rude to waiting staff.

ACTION/CONSIDERATION

When was the last time you complained about something? What happened?

Did you get the outcome you wanted? If not, how could you do it differently next time?

Can you think of any instances where you should have complained but didn't? What held you back?

What will help you to behave differently next time?

Practise out loud some ways of complaining politely that feel natural to you without apologising.

PEARL 16

Choose friends wisely

> *"Set your life on fire. Seek those who fan your flames."*
> **RUMI, SUFI POET AND MYSTIC**

When I was a teenager, my dad told me something that's stuck with me ever since. In my life, I would only ever have the number of close friends that I could count on one hand. In fact, probably only two or three fingers. Tops. At the time, I just thought Dad was a bit misguided because at the age of thirteen, of course, I knew everything. The fact that my dad had years of life experience and wisdom, accounted for absolutely nothing when I was a know-it-all teenager. But how right he was, bless his soul.

How your friends show up and step up for you in times of adversity is a pretty good barometer of the quality of the relationship you have with them. Friends will fall into different camps. The particular Pearl of Wisdom I want to share with you is that you need to *manage your own expectations* of your friends. Be realistic about what they bring to your relationship. I've learnt this the hard way. Thinking that someone will show up in a certain way or do something for me and then being massively disappointed when they let me down was a tough lesson. I needed to manage my own expectations of what that friend was like and what she was capable of or willing to do. And how ultimately that would change the nature of our relationship.

Actionable advice

There'll be friends, if you're lucky, who you *absolutely* know would get up in the middle of the night and travel across the country if you were in trouble. There'll be others who are less reliable, maybe for very good reasons, but who you have a lot of fun with and who bring you joy and make you laugh. There'll be friends who support and encourage you, who help you in your endeavours, whether that's with practical or emotional support. There'll be those who are able to be brutally honest with you when you're being a tit or you're on the road to self-destruction. It won't be all your friends who are willing or able to do all of these things. It's just important you understand what you get from your friendships. And, be very aware of any so-called friends who don't do *any* of these things for you.

Friendship's a funny thing. I was sitting in my garden last summer with my neighbour and she was telling me about a friend of hers. She wasn't very happy with the way this friend was treating her. I was shocked by some of the things she told me. It certainly wasn't how I'd define friendship. I asked how long she'd known this woman. "Oh... we were at school together."

"Ahah," I said. "That explains it." She looked at me quizzically. "This woman isn't your *friend*," I said. "Not now, anyway. She's a *habit*." And a bad habit at that. Friendships can go on being habitual until you question what you're getting out of it. Is this a two-way thing? I used to have a friend who never got in touch with me. I'd make the effort because when we *did* meet he was so funny and such good value it seemed worthwhile. Until it wasn't. I got fed up with always being the one who made the effort. I gave more than I got. And after a while, I gave up.

Is it time to look at your friendships and take stock of where you're at with some of them? Later on, we'll talk about choosing quality over quantity and there's no better place to start with *that* Pearl of Wisdom than friendships.

> *"You cannot change the people around you, but you can change the people you choose to be around."*
> **UNKNOWN**

Of course it's not just platonic relationships that can fall into this trap. A lot of couples are together not because they want to be, but because it's become a habit. Many long-married couples tolerate each other at best. I find that dreadfully sad. But equally, I know how hard leaving a marriage can be. It takes a lot of courage. People can get trapped by the standard of living they're used to. The huge emotional rollercoaster, the impact of separation on children, the guilt, the shame, the fear of failure, what other people will think. And the prospect of being on their own again can be frightening. There are many reasons to stay. If you're reading this and you're questioning the state of your relationship, I'll just share the one thing that kept haunting me. *I only have this one precious life.*

ACTION/CONSIDERATION

Do you have any friends who've become habits?

Name the person who tells you the uncomfortable things that you might not want to hear.

Name the person you could trust if your life really depended on it.

And who talks a good story but doesn't really step up when you need them?

Is there anything you need to say or do following these reflections?

PEARL 17

Become a better listener

> *"You cannot truly listen to anyone and do anything else at the same time."*
> **M. SCOTT PECK, PSYCHIATRIST AND AUTHOR**

If there's one skill we're piss poor at as a society, it's listening. In shops and on the phone to call centres, I seriously have to channel my inner zen when I'm having to repeat myself multiple times, because people can't be arsed to listen properly. Being a good listener is a super-skill. It'll stand you in good stead both in your personal and your professional life if you can master it. And as most people aren't good listeners, it will set you apart.

Years ago, I did some work on what made people charismatic. Listening and being present are two vital elements of charisma. And of course they're totally connected. You can't listen properly unless you're really present. The Chinese have a wonderful symbol for "listen" called *Ting*. The character is split into five parts which represent all the different aspects of good listening. The ears, the eyes, the mind and the heart. And at the centre of the character is a fifth single stroke which represents the need for total attention and focus. Being present. How you can you listen properly if your mind is somewhere else? I was on a Facetime call with a friend of mine the other day. We don't get to see each other often and she's always super busy. So she suggested we catch up while she was making a cake. I suggested instead that we reschedule when she was able to give her full attention to our time together.

So if you know you tend to get distracted, as we all do, maybe have a look at my thoughts on meditation (Pearl 23) because that will really help you become aware of how present you actually are.

Actionable advice

One of the reasons we're so poor at listening is that we're too busy thinking about what we're going to say next or how we're going to respond and so we miss stuff. We're not listening to be curious, we're often listening so we can say something about us that's relevant.

> *"Most people do not listen with the intent to understand; they listen with the intent to reply."*
> **STEPHEN R. COVEY, AUTHOR, BUSINESSMAN AND SPEAKER**

And often, we don't give the person we're talking to our undivided attention because we're doing something else at the same time. Hey, I'm guilty as charged but meditating has helped me become more present. I'm more self-aware now when I'm listening and trying not to interrupt! That's such an annoying habit. I really appreciate it in others when I can see they're making an effort to give me their undivided attention and not to interrupt.

I'm a big people watcher. I also find myself listening to other people's conversations, particularly on the train. But what's interesting is that mostly they're not *actually* conversations. They're just a trade of facts.

"Where are you going on holiday?"

"Oh, we're going to France."

"Oh yes, *we* went to France last year."

Most people bring the subject back to themselves rather than asking questions. If you can engage more with what the other person is actually saying, ask questions and resist the temptation to bring everything back to *you*, you'll be one step ahead of most people. The bonus of this approach is that whoever you're talking to will think you're great. Goes back to charisma.

> *"To be interesting, be interested."*
> **DALE CARNEGIE, AMERICAN WRITER**
> **AND LECTURER**

ACTION/CONSIDERATION

How would you rate yourself as a listener?
Do you interrupt?

What gets in the way of you fully listening?

What could you do to improve your listening skills?

What do you think the impact of this might be?

PEARL 18

....

Watch what people DO, not what they SAY

> *"You are what you do, not what you say you'll do."*
> **CARL JUNG, PSYCHIATRIST**
> **AND PSYCHOANALYST**

Actions speak louder than words. It's a cliché, but clichés are clichés for a reason. Because generally they're true and wise. The wisdom for you here is to note what people *do*, not what they *say* they'll do. I remember when I was starting out in the world of work and somewhat impressionable, I was definitely persuaded by silver-tongued professionals who talked a good story. As I've become older and more cynical, I listen to the words with interest but hold off judgement until I see the action to back it up. Some politicians have been shining examples of this. Lots of empty promises and zero action.

If your friends, colleagues, family members promise to do something, do they do it? Do they step up when you need them to? Or are they full of chat but when it comes to delivering on a promise they made to you they somehow disappear? Leaders in business who don't "walk their talk" are not as respected as those who demonstrate their values by action. Talk is cheap.

Actionable advice

Start to become aware of people either personally or professionally who you feel you can trust. And that's going to depend to a great degree on whether they do what they say they're going to do.

I was talking to a friend of mine about this the other day. He was telling me about an ex-girlfriend of his who always used the phrase *"I've got your back"*. Sounds great, doesn't it? Until he needed her to do something important for him. Then she miraculously had other priorities, namely herself, that were far more important. That was the straw that broke that relationship's back because he finally saw her in her true colours. We laughed about it because he said his intuition was ringing alarm bells right at the beginning of the relationship. But he ignored it. Clearly, his head, or maybe another part of his body, was running the show?!

The biggest piece of wisdom I can give you about committing to a relationship is to make sure your person walks their talk. When things are going well, you may not fully see this. It's only when the shit hits the fan that you see someone's true colours. How they react under stress or when things get emotionally tough is a real measure of their character. I always say travelling together is a good test of a relationship because sometimes things go a bit tits up and it can get stressy. You either start to blame each other, "well *you* booked this bloody hotel", or you come together and work as a team to manage the situation. When loved ones get sick or die you'll also see how your partner reacts. Do they stand by you or do they find it "too stressful" and just don't show up for you?

ACTION/CONSIDERATION

Are you aware of anyone who doesn't deliver on their promises?

Can you think of an example? What did they say? What did they do?

How are you going to deal with this?

PEARL 19

....

Let go of the idea that you can fix someone

> *"Stop trying to fix someone who doesn't actually want to be fixed."*
> **SASSY GODMOTHER, AUTHOR, SPEAKER AND SPIRITUAL ADVENTURER**

Trying to fix someone else's problems for them when they don't want it for themselves is a bloody waste of your precious time. And that's a valuable lesson to learn.

Years ago, I rented out the spare room in my London flat to a young woman I met at the local tennis club. Sometimes we'd sit and chat in the evenings. Actually, we didn't chat. She told me all her problems and I listened patiently, like the good coach-in-the-making I was trying to be. This went on for a while and I offered her tons of advice and potential solutions to the various issues and challenges she had in her life. Men, job, boss, la la la.

But as the months went by and nothing seemed to change for her, it began to dawn on me that I was ***totally wasting my time***. It took me a good while to realise this particular piece of wisdom. She kept saying things like "that's a great idea" or "yes, you're right". So I assumed she'd do something about it. But she didn't have the will or the desire to fix her problems. Nothing I could have said would have made a scrap of difference. Not only did she not have the will, desire or courage to make the changes, I realised that she was obviously getting something out of the time and attention I was devoting to her. Either consciously or subconsciously, on some level, it was serving her to be this victim of circumstance. And she clearly wasn't going to sort herself out. I was much more strongly in my masculine energy back then. So I was on a mission to try to "fix problems" and "find solutions" to help her deal with all her challenges. If I had the same situation occur today with the wisdom I have now, I'd politely listen but not invest too much energy.

Actionable advice

When you go into a new relationship, there'll be things that you might find challenging or frustrating about your partner. They may enrol you to help them fix something they don't like about themselves or a habit they're trying to build or break. That's great. There's at least a willingness to want to change. But if they don't change, you have to accept them as they are. Believing you can fix or change someone is a major route to unhappiness.

Many women are attracted by the "bad boy". The popular, good-looking rogue who's edgy and fun and somehow a little inaccessible. A bit of a challenge. There's a belief amongst some women that they can somehow change him. Mould him. Train him! This story usually ends in heartache and frustration. The bad boy is frequently emotionally unavailable and dislikes commitment. Fine if that's OK with you. Just know you're unlikely to be able to change his DNA. Far better for you to be on your own than with someone who isn't right for you and who you want to fix.

> "Travel alone if you must. The worst person to have with you is someone who isn't equally enchanted with the view."
> **SAMA AKBAR, HUMAN-POTENTIAL THOUGHT LEADER**

One final thought on this one and I'm going to use a cliché to describe it because it just sums it up so well. You can lead a horse to water, but you can't make it drink. Over the years, I've had many situations where I've offered to help people out where I can see they're struggling with something. I guess it comes with the territory of being a coach. It may have been offering up my time or putting them in touch with someone I know. The piece of wisdom I've learned is that I can offer these things til I'm blue in the face – and I used to waste a lot of time and energy following up. "Have you contacted so and so?" "The offer is still there if you want it…" What I've learned is that people will come to things in their own time – or they won't. And that's fine.

ACTION/CONSIDERATION

*Are you aware that you're trying to fix
or change someone?*

*Why do you think you're doing it? What evidence do
you have that they have changed – or haven't?*

*What can you do or say to yourself when you get the
urge to try to change someone?*

PEARL 20

....

Aim to be of service

"Everyone has a purpose in life and a unique talent to give to others. And when we blend this unique talent with service to others, we experience the ecstasy and exultation of our own spirit, which is the ultimate goal of all goals."
DR KALLAM ANJI REDDY, SCIENTIST, ENTREPRENEUR AND PHILANTHROPIST

We talked earlier about those unique gifts you've been given. You need to share them with the world, otherwise it's a waste. You have them for a reason. I firmly believe that finding your True Nature and using your talents and abilities to be of service to others is one of the main reasons we're here having this human experience. So what do I mean by "being of service"?

It's an attitude of mind, to use your gifts and abilities to benefit others. Another way I've heard this described is "shining your light". Don't be afraid to shine your light. I love that. Don't hide your light under that proverbial bushel.

Actionable advice

A couple of Buddhist principles which you might like to consider are not to harm others under any circumstances, and *to help others as much as possible*. This could be small acts of kindness or large gestures, whatever you're able to do. It might simply be helping an elderly person with their luggage on a train. Now more than ever, the world needs us to be kinder to each other. If you can take on board that in some extraordinary energetic way *we are all connected*, the more we help each other and are kinder to each other, the more beneficial it is for everyone. And obviously, a lot of people can't see it that way. But, the more of us that do, the better the world will be.

> *"When you help, you see life as weak. When you fix, you see life as broken. When you serve, you see life as whole. Fixing and helping may be the work of the ego, and service the work of the soul."*
> **RACHEL NAOMI REMEN, AUTHOR**

I just know from personal experience that the more I give of myself and the kinder I am, the richer my life is. Volunteering has proved to have substantial mental health benefits, including feeling part of the community and feeling good about giving. So how could you give either more of yourself, your time or your resources? And watch what happens.

Your intention around this is important, though. Being kind and compassionate in a *non-conditional way*, just for the hell of it and not expecting anything back, is a good way to approach it.

> *"Even after all this time*
> *The Sun never says to the earth*
> *'You owe me'*
> *Look what happens with a love like that*
> *It lights up the whole sky."*
> **HAFIZ, SUFI POET**
> **THE SUN NEVER SAYS**

And in your professional life, you'll have a customer or a client or someone you're working for. It could be an internal client. How could you serve them better? What more could you give of yourself? This is not about being powerless to your customers' unrealistic demands or having no boundaries about how much time you put in, but about aiming to be of service more often when the opportunity presents itself.

> *"A customer is the most important visitor on our premises.*
> *He is not dependent on us. We are dependent on him. He is*
> *not an interruption of our work. He is the purpose of it. He*
> *is not an outsider of our business. He is part of it. We are*
> *not doing him a favour by serving him. He is doing us a*
> *favour by giving us the opportunity to do so."*
> **MAHATMA GANDHI, LAWYER, ANTI-COLONIAL**
> **NATIONALIST AND ETHICIST**

ACTION/CONSIDERATION

*Where could you be of more service in your life?
Personally? Professionally?*

What gifts do you have that you could share?

How does it feel to be genuinely "of service"?

PEARL 21

....

Pay it forward

> *"A single act of kindness throws out roots in all directions,*
> *and the roots spring up and make new trees."*
> **AMELIA EARHART, AVIATION PIONEER**
> **AND WRITER**

And closely linked to being of service is one of the most wonderful things you can do to really feed your soul. And it's been proven to radically boost mental health. Something so simple as just *connecting more with other people*.

And that includes people you don't know. Take it a step further and think about embracing the idea of *"paying it forward"*. This idea first came to light in a book published over a hundred years ago. And more recently it was the subject of another book entitled *Pay It Forward* which was subsequently made into a film of the same name. It stars Kevin Spacey and Haley Joel Osment and I'd highly recommend you watch it. A school teacher played by Spacey challenges twelve-year-old Osment to come up with a concept that'll change the world. The boy decides he'll help three people with an act of kindness. He then urges those three people to help *another* three people and so on and so on, making a social movement by all the acts of kindness.

Actionable advice

You can practise random acts of kindness which require no conditions at all. Just do something for the pure joy of knowing you've helped someone, which can be totally anonymous. The US celebrate Random Acts of Kindness Day on the 17th February by the way, and Pay it Forward Day is April 30th. *Who knew?!*

> *"Kindness is a language which the deaf can hear and the blind can see."*
> **MARK TWAIN, WRITER, LECTURER, HUMOURIST AND ESSAYIST**

Being kind and considerate can be highly contagious. Carrying out random acts of kindness to strangers can have a massive ripple effect. It's been shown that if one car driver gives way to another to get out of a side road, it's highly likely that the second driver will let someone else out at some point.

I get great pleasure from giving compliments to strangers: on the street, on the tube. Just striking up a conversation in a café or a restaurant, or frankly anywhere you find yourself. It's very un-British but it can lead to some wonderful interactions, like seeing people's faces when you pay them an unexpected compliment. They probably think I'm barking, but, frankly, I don't mind that one bit.

> *"The best way to find joy is to give it to others."*
> **ROBERT G. INGERSOLL, AMERICAL LAWYER, WRITER AND ORATOR**

ACTION/CONSIDERATION

If you think of the various aspects of your life and your regular schedule, to which areas could you introduce random acts of kindness?

Could you do it regularly? Make it a habit?

Could you treat a habitually annoying situation with kindness instead?

PEARL 22

....

Prioritise joy

> *"Find out where joy resides, and give it a voice far beyond singing. For to miss the joy is to miss all."*
> **ROBERT LOUIS STEVENSON, SCOTTISH NOVELIST AND ESSAYIST**

One of the things I've learned as I've got older is how important it is to prioritise joy. Simply working out what it is you love doing and making sure you're doing it on a regular basis seems so obvious, doesn't it? But do you do it enough? Why are so many of us not spending more time doing the things that bring us joy? Too busy doing stuff we "have" to do rather than things we "want" to do? Children have the most wonderful capacity to see joy in so much of life but we adults can get bogged down by our responsibilities and taking life and ourselves far too seriously.

*

Many years ago, I went on an energy course in Glastonbury run by a wonderful man called William Bloom.* You might want to check William out. He's one of the UK's leading teachers in mind, body and spirit. He's written a number of books and was co-founder of the Alternatives organisation at St James's Church in Piccadilly in London. As we sat on the floor in a circle, one of the first things William asked us to do was think about our strawberries.

Strawberries?

Actionable advice

Very simply, in William's wonderful metaphor, strawberries are the things you love doing, the people you love being with and the places you love to be. This simple piece of wisdom has stayed with me all these years. And as I've got older, I've realised just how important it is to identify what these are and make sure you spend enough of your precious time on your strawberries and less on other things which aren't so nourishing. This is about a bodily sensation, an endorphin effect that these activities create inside you.

I had an example of this when I went on a jazz cruise last year. Live jazz feeds my soul like nothing else. For me, it's a big, fat, plump, red strawberry. And funnily enough, although I've always loved jazz and gone to gigs and concerts all my life, it never really dawned on me *how much* it feeds me, until recently. I went on the cruise on my own (you have to be a real jazz head to want to have seven solid days pretty much 24/7, so my partner stayed at home). We were having a WhatsApp call while I was sitting on my bed in my cabin floating somewhere round the Caribbean. He said how sparkly my eyes looked, how I was fizzing with energy and how much joy and happiness was radiating out of me. I realised in that moment how much this literally *was* nourishing my soul. And it was manifesting itself physically. Needless to say, I've booked again for next year.

Some people refer to their "happy place". Now that could be an *actual* place, a physical location or it could be a situation where certain conditions are present. Let me give you examples of my strawberries so you can think about what yours might be.

A really good foot massage (frankly, any good massage), the mellow feeling after a sauna, being around animals, a particularly good glass of Rioja or Californian Chardonnay, lying in the sun (add in the live jazz and the glass of Chardonnay and you'll understand why I'm back on that jazz cruise next year), cuddling up on the sofa, eating a really tasty meal, walking in a quiet forest, watching the birds feeding and bathing in the garden, cooking a meal dancing round the kitchen, singing, hanging out with friends who make me laugh and who understand me, playing a really good game of tennis then collapsing into a hot, bubbly bath, my morning mug of tea in bed, driving my Z4 through the countryside with the roof down on a sunny day. This isn't rocket science but the general idea is to *do more* of the stuff that brings you joy and less of other stuff. Sometimes you just need to be more aware of what these things actually are for *you*. It's about being more *intentional* with how you spend your precious time.

I remember years ago my closest friend was staying with me for a few days in the summer. I had a cottage on the village green and she was sitting out at the front watching me as I left to go and play a tennis match. On my return a few hours later, she said something which got me thinking. "You looked like you were going off to do a job which you don't particularly enjoy." I'd been playing competitive tennis since I was a young kid, I'd been coached to within an inch of my life, played tournaments, it was just *what I did.*

But where was the joy?

We can get so caught up in our habitual routines that we don't sometimes stop to question *why* we're doing something. If we've always done it, we can carry on regardless without questioning whether it's actually bringing us any joy or not.

I did stop playing tennis for about ten years after two keyhole surgeries on my hip. I didn't miss it that much. It was clearly time for a break. About three years ago, I started playing again but the difference is I'm enjoying it far more now. I won't let it get to the point where it becomes joyless ever again. The same happened with my candle business side hustle. When it ceased to be fun and joyful, I stopped doing it.

And the other thing is, joy doesn't have to be *expensive*. Mother nature has a terrific array of joyful goodies for us to immerse ourselves in. If we get our heads out of our phones from time to time, we can see what beauty and joy is all around us. Just becoming more conscious in seeking it out is all you have to do.

ACTION/CONSIDERATION

What are the things that you love doing? What nourishes your soul?

Who are the people you love hanging out with? Can you identify why?

Where are the places that make you feel good?

What was the best holiday or weekend away you've ever had? Where were you? What were you doing? Who were you with?

Are you doing anything out of habit or obligation that doesn't actually bring you any joy?

Where can you increase the level of joy in your life? Where can you create more time for your strawberries?

PEARL 23

....

Understand what meditation is and why it's so good for you

> "The goal of mediation is not to get rid of thoughts or emotions. The goal is to become more aware of your thoughts and emotions and learn how to move through them without getting stuck."
>
> **DR PHILIPPE R. GOLDIN, PROFESSOR OF CLINICAL NEUROSCIENCE, UNIVERSITY OF CALIFORNIA, DAVIS**

OK, so we've already said that one of the ways to grow as a person is to understand yourself better. Hang out with yourself more often. The way I've done it is to practise meditation every day. This means I'm carving out some time alone every single morning.

Now, I have to warn you. There's a huge amount of bullshit around meditation. And a lot of misunderstanding about what meditation actually *is* and how you do it. It's become much more mainstream in the last twenty years or so. Which is great, don't get me wrong. But some people want to make it prescriptive and mysterious. Something which is basically very simple is in danger of becoming complicated and intimidating. There's also loads of different types of meditation out there. I'm just going to give you my take on it, tell you what I do every day and what the benefits are. And I'm not saying my way is the *right* way. It's *a* way. And it's straightforward. But you'll need to see what works for you.

Actionable advice

Firstly, find a place where you're comfy. Every morning I sit in my meditation chair in my study. If you try and do it at roughly the same time, in the same place every day, you'll have a *much better chance of building a habit*. So gently rest your gaze on a point just in front of you. Notice yourself breathing in and out. If you haven't done this before, I'd suggest trying it with your eyes open as you'll stand more chance of staying present. I think if you shut your eyes you're more likely to nod off or drift off into your thoughts and to-do list. Play around with it and see what works best for you. For me, meditation isn't about drifting off or falling asleep. You need to be relaxed and comfy, but all your senses need to be activated and you need to *be present*.

> *"In mindfulness one is not only restful and happy, but alert and awake. Meditation is not evasion; it is a serene encounter with reality."*
> **THICH NHAT HANH, ZEN MASTER,**
> **SPIRITUAL LEADER**

So you hear the noises but you don't judge them. When I was first with my partner and I announced I was off to meditate, he said he'd creep around quietly. He was a bit surprised when I said, "Don't worry, be as noisy as you like." You should be able to meditate anywhere and anytime. And that includes Piccadilly Circus at rush hour. It's simply about observing your thoughts while staying present.

And let's just talk about "being present" for a moment. You'll have heard a lot about this in the last few years. It's *hugely* important. For lots of reasons. Being present is *about paying attention in the present moment in a non-judgemental way with all your five senses activated*, so being completely in touch and aware of the present moment. Your meditation is simply the practice of taking time to be present. And the general idea is that by meditating more, you start to train yourself to be more present for more of the day.

> *"Do not dwell in the past, do not dream of the future, concentrate the mind on the present moment."*
> **BUDDHA, RELIGIOUS TEACHER**

This means being conscious of what you're doing in each moment. Essentially, you're not operating on autopilot like most of us are most of the time. When you put your keys down and you can't remember where you put them it's because you weren't actually "there" when you put your keys down. You were thinking about something else. The idea is that you rest your attention in the present moment, in the now, when you're going through your daily activities. Like eating your breakfast or cleaning your teeth. So you're not thinking about the past or planning the future but you're simply *being here now.* Just noticing and observing. Not judging yourself or others in this process. And then you start to appreciate the world around you a lot more because you become more *aware.* You get your head out of your phone and you start to engage with the world. And that's when your quality of your life starts to change and you start to appreciate being alive. And you become less anxious.

> *"The ability to be in the present moment is a major component of mental wellness."*
> **ABRAHAM MASLOW, PSYCHOLOGIST**

One of the biggest myths about meditation is that you should somehow stop thinking. Well, that just ain't going to happen. You can't stop your heart beating and you can't stop your mind thinking. Meditation isn't about you clearing your mind. You'll still have thoughts. The trick is not to get carried away with your thoughts. The way I describe it – it's a bit like standing on a platform. Think about the train as a thought. Just don't get on the train. Let it pass and observe it.

And also, rather than seeing your thoughts as the enemy, try seeing them as your *guests.* And just *observe* them. Stay in the present moment and be aware of your body, notice your feet on the floor and where your hands are resting. Remember, this isn't about trying to clear your mind. It's about noticing what's *there.*

Try it for five minutes and see how you get on. I'd recommend you use an app like Insight Timer so you don't need to worry about timing yourself. You can set it to ping at various intervals and as you get more into it, you can do more. I do twenty minutes daily but I've been doing it for quite a while.

It's obvious from all the research that the benefits of practising this stuff are as long as your arm. And mine.

> *"Meditation is like a gym in which you develop the*
> *powerful mental muscles of calm and insight."*
> ***AJAHN BRAHM, BUDDHIST MONK***

For starters, it'll improve your concentration levels enormously. It's a bit like taking your mind to the gym. You'll find it easier to focus because meditating is about being present and you're building that habit. Another big plus is that meditation is really good at strengthening your nervous system. After all, for much of the time you're walking around in a state of high alert. We're constantly bombarded by a huge amount of negative stimuli. Add this to the day-to-day stresses of life, and that puts quite a strain on your nervous system. So when you get triggered by someone or something, it's likely that you'll react emotionally. If you're more mindful, you'll be able to take a pause and do what Buddhists call *"recognising the spark before the flame"*. This means you can respond, rather than react. And this is a very useful skill to have.

I can tell you I've calmed and slowed down a hell of a lot since I started meditating. I take a much more measured approach to life and I'm convinced it's because I take time every day to sit in my chair and just *be*. I still get triggered when someone in a Range Rover drives straight at me in the middle of a country lane. But hey ho, I do it less. And I'm very aware I'm doing it. Which is progress. Remember, this is a journey.

And when you start taking time and space to simply *observe* your thoughts, you'll get much clearer on what you're fixating on. You may even begin to realise that you aren't your thoughts. And then you can choose whether you keep those thoughts and beliefs, or let them go.

> *"Don't believe everything you think.*
> *Thoughts are just that – thoughts."*
> **ALLAN LOKOS, FOUNDER AND GUIDING**
> **TEACHER OF THE COMMUNITY**
> **MEDITATION CENTRE, NYC**

And here's something else you might find useful. Get others involved in supporting you when you start meditating. To be honest, it's as much about managing other people's expectations as anything else. Over the years, my partners have just accepted that my twenty-minute meditation is non-negotiable wherever I am in the world. One of my clients even got her kids to join in. Getting your family or partner to help you build a habit can be a smart move. And that doesn't just apply to meditation.

And don't worry, because when you start meditating, it'll frustrate the living fuck out of you. I can promise you now, your mind will tear off all over the place. You'll feel fidgety, antsy and you'll want to stop. Just accept it and gently bring your attention back to your gaze. And you know what? Let go of the idea of doing it "perfectly" or "doing it right". Remember, there's a massive difference between *simple* and *easy*. Is this simple? Yes. Is it easy? Hell, no. It's taken me twenty years to get my arse in my chair every day. And I still have days when my mind's behaving like a rowdy two-year-old. But let me tell you, it's worth it. On so many levels. I'd really encourage you to give it a go. See it as a gift to yourself. Just keep turning up to your chair or your comfy space every day. This on its own is a masterclass in self-discipline. Just don't get hung up on the outcome.

> *"It is indeed a radical act of love just to sit down and be quiet for a time by yourself."*
> **JON KABAT-ZINN, PROFESSOR EMERITUS OF MEDICINE, UNIVERSITY OF MASSACHUSETTS**

ACTION/CONSIDERATION

How do you feel about the idea of starting a meditation practice?

Can you feel any resistance?

Where in your living space could you create a comfortable and appropriate place to meditate?

When would be the best time for you to meditate?

Can your partner or family help you to build a habit?

PEARL 24

Exercise gratitude regularly

> *"If the only prayer you ever say in your entire life is thank you, it will be enough."*
> **MEISTER ECKHART, CATHOLIC THEOLOGIAN, PHILOSOPHER AND MYSTIC**

When I sit in my meditation chair every morning, I take the time to thank the Universal Mind – or whatever you want to call it – for all the goodies I currently have in my life. I also say thank you in advance for sending me all the things that are for my highest good. All the things that will help me get back to my True Nature. This could be the right people, situations, opportunities or resources coming my way. I give thanks in advance for parking spaces to be available, for weekends and holidays to flow, for restaurants to have tables, for bars to have bar stools! And in places where you can't book, it's uncanny how we always seem to get a table. Or the last two seats at the bar or a parking space just where we need it. And I always say thank you. Even my partner has given up on the idea that it's just a coincidence because it happens so often. He asks me to do my "witchy thing" when we need a parking space or a table in a crowded café! It seems to me that, in some vibrational way, the more you exercise gratitude on a regular basis, the more you strengthen your connection to the universal energy field.

Actionable advice

You don't need to meditate to say thank you on a more regular basis. It could be during the day for absolutely anything. When clients pay money into my account, when I get a 3 for 2 on something that I just happened to want to buy, it makes me smile and I say thank you. You can start doing more of that right now. Start with a heartfelt thank you for what you have in your life. Being thankful when you open your eyes in the morning for another new day. To be grateful that you're alive and well. Not everyone has that luxury. Look for opportunities when things go right to acknowledge it. Say thanks – you noticed.

> *"When you arise in the morning think of what a privilege it is to be alive, to think, to enjoy, to love."*
> **MARCUS AURELIUS, ROMAN EMPEROR AND STOIC PHILOSOPHER**

I'm a jazz head. And when I hear a really good busker that lifts my spirits, I clap and give them a few quid. *Because.* Of course I'm mostly the only one on the London Underground who's clapping but that's OK. Gratitude can be a willingness to show others you appreciate their efforts. Whether it's a busker or someone cleaning the loos in a bar or restaurant, a "thank you", whether it's spoken or comes from your purse, ideally both, is just a lovely thing to do. A great busker can really lift your mood and a thank you and a couple of quid can really lift theirs. The more you do this, the more you exercise your "Gratitude Muscle". And it makes you feel good about yourself. What's not to like?

> *"Feeling gratitude and not expressing it is like wrapping a present and not giving it."*
> **WILLIAM ARTHUR WARD, AMERICAN MOTIVATIONAL WRITER**

ACTION/CONSIDERATION

When in your life do you habitually show gratitude?

When have you felt it and not expressed it?

Where in your life could you exercise gratitude more regularly?

PEARL 25

....

Soothe yourself with just being

> *"In today's rush, we all think too much, want too much,*
> *and forget about the joy of just being."*
> **ECKHART TOLLE, SPIRITUAL TEACHER AND**
> **SELF-HELP AUTHOR**

If you were to ask me the word that describes the feeling of just sitting and being, ideally in peaceful, quiet surroundings, I'd say the word "soothe". It's as if a wonderful wave of peace and tranquillity engulfs me and I'm just being *soothed*. In a world of increasing speed, noise, action, stress and distraction, the *ultimate* antidote is just to be still and calm.

And yet, how many of us actually ever do that? Especially us women. Apart from sleeping, when did you last sit or lie and do precisely nothing? Never? Can't remember? And actually – can you even do it? And I don't count "nothing" as being tied to an electronic gadget. That's not doing nothing. Sometimes you just need to *stop doing anything at all*. And that's hard. Most of us are inherently uncomfortable with the idea of "not doing" anything. It can provoke enormous amounts of anxiety and guilt. We're just not programmed that way. It somehow feels counter-intuitive and indulgent. Lazy even? You'll *worry* that you're not doing anything or being "productive". And then you'll feel guilty.

We live in a society where "being busy" seems to have become a badge of honour. And it's been that way for a while. If anyone used to ask my mum how she was, her stock answer was "busy". I grew up thinking this was the sign of success. Busyness. A productive, happy life. *Not necessarily so* is what'd I'd say to you now. As a culture, we're far too busy. I can sense a slight backlash starting to emerge. Post-Covid, people started to reassess their work-life balance to provide more space and time for themselves. Which is great. But as a society, I think we're still way out of balance.

Actionable advice

If you start with your body, your mind will eventually follow. So if you can, at some point during your week, find somewhere to sit or lie where you're comfy and just allow the stillness and quiet to wash over you like a wave. Just soothe your body and mind in the wonder and joy of doing nothing. You're sending yourself a message that it's OK to just shut down physical and mental activity for a short time and just *be*.

> *"Almost everything will work again if you unplug it for a few minutes, including you."*
> **ANNE LAMOTT, NOVELIST, POLITICAL ACTIVIST AND SPEAKER**

These phases are important. But in your busy life, you have to *make a conscious decision* to carve out time to be. Otherwise it won't happen. If you commute, maybe just put your tech away and allow your mind to drift. To wander aimlessly and bimble about. Try for a short period – say five or ten minutes – and just see how it feels. See what you notice.

> *"A daily dose of daydreaming heals the heart, soothes the*
> *soul, and strengthens the imagination."*
> **HENRY DAVID THOREAU, NATURALIST,**
> **ESSAYIST, POET AND PHILOSOPHER**

If you're always on the go, running from one thing to another, doing, doing, doing, ask yourself, "why?" What are you avoiding? You've also got to recognise that you can't be upbeat, motivated and in "go" mode all of the time. You fundamentally need to allow yourself time to rest, recalibrate, reassess things and reflect. If you never grant yourself this gift, you slowly start to become like a volcano that could erupt at any time. If this happens, it's going to stress you out. Your batteries need recharging. So allow yourself the time to come home to yourself every once in a while.

Why don't you have a go at resisting those thoughts of laziness and guilt in the moments where you'd actually like to do nothing? And just enjoy it. Go on – humour me. Just try it. Just see if you *can* lie on the sofa for five minutes and do bugger all. Remember, no phone allowed. What happens?

> "Be still. The quieter you become, the more you can hear."
> **RAM DASS, SPIRITUAL TEACHER AND WRITER**

ACTION/CONSIDERATION

Do you ever truly allow yourself to just be?

What happens when you think about stopping every so often and doing nothing?

What thoughts and feelings come up?

PEARL 26

....

Uni-task and slow down

> *"He who pursues everything achieves nothing."*
> **FICINO, SCHOLAR AND CATHOLIC PRIEST,**
> **BOOK 2 LETTER 30, 10ᵀᴴ DECEMBER 1476**

What Ficino was saying and Plato before him plays out today in our obsessive desire to do multiple things at once. And I'm guilty as charged. But increasingly, I'm trying *not to*. And I'd urge you to have a go at doing the same.

I coined the phrase "uni-task" as my alternative to multitasking. Why? Because I'm simply not convinced that trying to do multiple things at once *actually works* in the long run. When you're not putting 100% of your whole attention on something, I don't think you do it 100% properly. Now, I'm not talking about seeking perfection here. I'm talking about focusing on one thing at a time so you can do it to the best of your ability. And then you can move on to your next task.

Actionable advice

When I've encouraged clients to take this more focused "do one thing at a time" approach, they've really seen the benefits. Ironically, in some cases, they've found they've done a task well *and* quicker by not getting distracted by other plates they're spinning. This takes a bit of self-discpline. It's very tempting to want to juggle three or four things at once, thinking you'll get more done.

Time and time again, I've sent e-mails to people who clearly don't read them properly because they're in too much of a hurry. They come back with half an answer and then we waste time going back and forth with more e-mails trying to get the whole story. If they'd read it properly in the first place, that wouldn't have happened. Now I know I'm in danger of sounding like a grumpy old woman here… but I firmly believe that doing one thing at a time thoroughly is actually more productive in the longer term.

> *"In a world addicted to speed, slowness is a superpower."*
> **CARL HONORÉ, JOURNALIST AND AUTHOR**

In the same spirit as getting comfortable with just sitting and being, you're probably going to roll your eyes at my suggestion of slowing down just a teeny bit. Being busy **and** being in a rush have become our norm. We pack too much in and we're constantly rushing to get to where we need to be next. Is it me or is that stressful?

The biggest problem with rushing around all the time is that you're actually creating a bio-feedback loop with your stress chemicals. You know your mind and body are two completely interconnected systems? Get in a powerful, grounded and relaxed physical state before doing a high-pressure presentation and you're sending the right messages to your brain. If you're constantly rushing around in a state of busyness and frantic activity, you're actually triggering stress hormones and making yourself worse. Walk around in a calmer, slower way, doing one thing at a time and you'll trigger a different response.

ACTION/CONSIDERATION

Where could you do things a little more slowly and deliberately in your life?

In what aspects of your daily life do you typically try and do multiple things at once?

How could you change that?

What would you need to say to yourself to remind you?

PEARL 27

....

Measure twice, cut once

> *"...fools rush in where angels fear to tread."*
> **ALEXANDER POPE, ENGLISH POET,**
> **TRANSLATOR AND SATIRIST FROM**
> **'AN ESSAY ON CRITICISM'**
>
> **(TURNED INTO A SONG BY JOHNNY MERCER**
> **MANY CENTURIES LATER)**

Very much connected to the idea of slowing down is this little
gem of a Pearl. Wise tailors, woodworkers and carpenters
up and down the country live and die by this one simple
mantra: measure twice, cut once. And I love it because it's
as much a metaphor for your life as it is for cutting valuable
pieces of fabric, wood, or carpet. Make sure you prepare and
measure thoroughly so you don't waste valuable materials
and resources by having to do it again. You can apply that
to anything.

Actionable advice

Part of the knock-on effect of being busy and time-poor is that it's very easy to rush into decisions without thinking through the consequences. Our impatience can overrride good old fashioned common sense. The "measure twice" principle is designed to bring exactly that to a process or decision – some element of measure, a braking mechanism. Make sure you get it right (as much as you can) before committing. And this could apply to absolutely anything. The resources you're most likely to waste in life by rushing in and making unnecessary mistakes are your precious time and money. Time is the most valuable resource you have. And believe me, the older you get, the more that's the case.

> *"Act in haste, repent at leisure."*
> **WILLIAM CONGREVE, ENGLISH PLAYWRIGHT,**
> **POET AND WHIG POLITICIAN**

ACTION/CONSIDERATION

Think of a time you leapt straight into something without preparing or thinking of the consequences.

What happened?

What could you have avoided?

What would you do differently in future?

PEARL 28

Follow Your North Star

> *"Until I understand where I am, I can't get to where I am going. This is the value of a compass when we are out walking or hiking and need to know we're going in the right direction. But we also have an internal North Star. It's that little nudge that tells us if we are on the right path to fulfilling our potential, or on the wrong path wasting energy traveling somewhere we don't need to go. So my advice to you is, pull out that compass every once in a while and make sure you are navigating in the right direction on your journey."*
>
> **JOHN C. MAXWELL, AUTHOR,**
> **SPEAKER AND PASTOR**

When you look up on a starry night, you'll see the North Star, Polaris, shining out like a beacon. This Pearl of Wisdom is about having a bright shining beacon that you can always locate. It reminds you of what *you're* doing and where *you're* going. The reasoning behind having a clear North Star is to firmly root you back into your own set of values, aspirations and your direction of travel.

OK, so earlier we talked about following your True Nature. Many people use the term "following your North Star" as finding your purpose in life. The way I talk about it is a *shorter- or medium-term goal or ambition* you have. Which maybe *part* of you following your True Nature. It could be a project you're working on, a qualification you're studying for, a job or promotion you're aiming for, an achievement you have in mind, a book or paper you're writing, finding a home, starting or adding to your family, it could be anything.

Actionable advice

I think it's worth spending a bit of time getting clear on what your current North Star is. What are your short- and medium-term goals and ambitions? It provides you with an anchor when you get blown off course. Other people's beliefs and opinions and the stuff the media feed you can distract you away from your North Star. If you have a constant that you can continually return to, it'll give you that strong foundation.

I think the most important reason for understanding what your North Star is, is that it gives you clear focus. It helps you make decisions about how to spend your time and money. You have a reason to say 'No' to the things that move you further away from that star and a big fat YES to those things that move you closer. So the wisdom here is to keep asking yourself the question: "does this move me closer to, or further away from, my North Star?" And I suspect you'll know the answer to that fairly instinctively.

ACTION/CONSIDERATION

··

*When I talk about your 'North Star', what do you
immediately think of?*

*What are you doing right now that's moving you
closer to your North Star?*

*Are you doing anything that's moving you
further away?*

*Thinking about that, what do you need to change to
keep yourself on course?*

PEARL 29

....

Say "hello" to your resistance

So, have you ever noticed sometimes that when you decide to do something really important or life-changing, there'll be a part of you that feels it'd be far better *not* to do that thing? And when that thing you want to do involves going out of your comfort zone, that part of you will become *even more insistent* that it's really not a good idea?

When this happens, you're experiencing something called Resistance. Resistance is the fear that stops us all doing the things we want to do. The thing about Resistance is that the more your heart and soul want to do something, the stronger it'll show up. The more you try and follow your North Star and your True Nature, the higher the chance that Resistance will rear its ugly head.

We all experience Resistance. It's how we're hardwired as humans. Our primeval limbic survival mechanism instinctively wants to protect us from harm, shame, embarrassment and anything else that makes us feel uncomfortable. It wants to keep us safe and cosy. It wants us to avoid risk. But it's also keeping us small. And the cost is that we never grow. And that's kinda the point of being here. Unfortunately, it's in direct conflict with the prefrontal cortex which is the logical, deep-thinking part of the brain, the wise bit.

OK, now for a bit of psychological history. It was good old Freud who picked up on the concept of resistance when many of his patients weren't getting better. He had a dream where he saw that his patient *didn't actually want* to get better or improve. Remember my flatmate a few chapters ago? Freud dedicated much of his work to analysing this "resistance".

Resistance can show up in all kinds of disguises and in all kinds of behaviours. Do you ever find yourself procrastinating? Constantly striving for perfection? Always thinking you need more time, more skills, more qualifications, more information? If the answer to any of these things is Yes, chances are, you're experiencing Resistance.

> *"Don't wait. The time will never be just right."*
> *NAPOLEON HILL, SELF-HELP AUTHOR*

Actionable advice

The trick is to be *self-aware* enough to understand how this Resistance shows up for *you*. I remember when I first started writing, I thought my house needed a deep clean and a good clear-out before I could start. My Resistance shows up as needing everything to be perfectly in order before I start. But ridiculously so. Procrastination on steroids. Procrastination is one of the biggest ways Resistance manifests itself in our lives. And we can become very good at rationalising it and believing it. But don't be fooled. And bear this very useful quote in mind:

> *"A year from now you may wish you'd started today."*
> **KAREN LAMB, AUTHOR, ARTIST, ILLUSTRATOR**

One of the ways of handling Resistance is to start building a relationship with it. That might sound crazy but what I've found works well is if you actually treat it as a *thing*. Observe yourself and start to see the Resistance for precisely what it is. You need to understand what it *is* so you don't go mistaking it for the truth. Say "hello" to it. Recognise it. Resistance is fear. It's part of your shadow side. It's trying to protect you from failure. The wiser part of you needs to be able to talk to it, comfort it and continue regardless. So you may experience this kind of internal battle. The wise part of you knows what you want to be doing. Resistance is trying to keep you safe and small in your cosy comfort zone. And it's clever. It'll feed you all kinds of convincing bullshit. One of the reasons meditation is so important is that it gives you the quiet time and space to see this fear for what it is. You can start to see this shadow side of yourself and to forgive yourself.

But of course, there's a caveat here. Sometimes you'll be resisting something for a bloody good reason. Your intuition might be warning you of something that's not in your best interests. How you distinguish between your intuitive voice and the voice of Resistance is going to be down to your ability to get to know your Resistance better. You need to be able to recognise it when it rears its head. The key is understanding *how* it shows up for you. What are the distinguishing feelings or behaviours it triggers in you? Like my sudden desire to clean the house from top to toe. Then you can have a conversation with it. "I know who you are and I know what you're trying to do, but I've got this covered and I know what I'm doing. It's OK." When it showed up for me, I just had to have a little word with myself. I had to reassure that part of me that writing was good and I was just going to get on with it and face the consequences of success or failure.

And talking of writing: another way of dealing with Resistance is to embrace the simple idea that *consistency* is a winner. Ask anyone who writes for a living and they'll probably tell you that the key to getting stuff done is to consistently turn up at the laptop or the pad and write a certain number of words every day or at least most of the days of the week. I certainly agree with that. Jeffrey Archer's writing regime is intense. He carves up his day into multiple two-hour time slots, but just look at how much he churns out. Writing intensely for two weeks and then doing bugger all for months is not a recipe for getting a book finished.

You'll triumph in building new habits if you can commit to doing five minutes of something every day – whether that's meditation, a practice of some sort, a household chore, an addition to the diet or exercise routine, *anything*. It could just be one minute. The idea being that instead of doing something very intensely every now and again, you do something a little more gently but more regularly. One glass of water in the morning, every morning. Something small, but just do it every day. Little and often. Repetition and consistency rather than erratic outbursts of intense activity every now and again.

> *"If you add a little to a little and do this often, soon the little will become great."*
> **HESIOD, ANCIENT POET**

Perfectionism can be a blocker to building a habit and doing something you want to do. I found this with singing. I thought I ought to be perfect at it straight away and that I really shouldn't have to practise. The real truth of it was that I was scared I wouldn't be good enough. But if the best opera singers in the world practise every day, then duh.

> *"If you want to master a habit, the key is to start with repetition, not perfection."*
> **JAMES CLEAR, AUTHOR**

You have a choice. You can go along with Resistance as your truth *or* you can rise above it, understand it's *not* the truth and let it go. The good thing about Resistance is that it's a very useful barometer for you. The more you're ***actually on the right track***, going down the right path, the more it will try to stop you.

ACTION/CONSIDERATION

How does Resistance show up for you?

What barriers and excuses do you put in place to rationalise your way out of doing what your heart really wants to do?

What one thing are you struggling to turn into a habit?

Where could you apply the little-and-often idea?

PEARL 30

....

Do the tough stuff first

> *"Delaying gratification is a process of scheduling the pain and pleasure of life in such a way as to enhance the pleasure by meeting and experiencing the pain first and getting it over with. It is the only decent way to live."*
>
> **M. SCOTT PECK, PSYCHIATRIST AND AUTHOR**

When I was a kid, I used to come home from school and plonk myself down on the floor in front of the TV. I would remain there, glued to the children's programmes starting with *Play School* at 3.55pm until *The Magic Roundabout* just before the early evening news. Children's programmes back in the day were truly awesome – I can still appreciate some of them as an adult. My long-suffering mum, meanwhile, would bring me a plate of sandwiches and some cakes while I was transfixed by the screen. The cakes would usually include a chocolate cupcake with thick chocolate icing on top of a round chocolate sponge wrapped in shiny silver paper. Being the impatient child I was, I would take off the chocolate icing, smash it into pieces (go figure) and then eat it, before devouring the sponge, which was the less appealing of the two.

Actionable advice

"So what?" you might think. Well, herein lies an interesting psychological phenomenon. It's called Delaying Gratification* and it really is a thing. And if you know you procrastinate, this is something worth thinking about.

Now you might not think that eating the icing first is a heinous crime when you're ten years old. Or that describing the sponge as "tough stuff" is entirely accurate, but it showed a lot about my behaviour as a child, particularly my preference for always choosing the fun stuff first. Always impatient. Wanting everything now. Play now, pay later.

And as I've got older, I've come to realise that life is far more enjoyable if I do the less preferable stuff first. It then frees me up to choose more favourable activities for the rest of my time. An hour or two of "pain" to enjoy six hours of pleasure! If you do it the other way round, there's a good chance that the "tough stuff" won't actually ever get done. It goes back to self-discipline and self-mastery and how you decide to schedule your time, whether you're at home or at work. If you operate any kind of to-do list, whether it's in your head, on paper or on a device you'll make a decision about which order you're going to do things. The temptation is to go for the "low-hanging fruit" and do the easy, quick stuff first to make you feel good. You feel like you're making progress as you cross it off your list. But next time you find yourself in this situation, why not try to flip it and do the less preferable or more time-consuming thing first? And then see how that makes you feel?

PEARL 31

See acceptance as a superpower

This is a biggie. I think being able to accept situations as they are is key to reducing your stress levels. Don't fight the current reality if you can't control it. It's a waste of your precious time and energy. Understand you have the power to change the things you can and be accepting of those things you can't change. This is one of the biggest pieces of wisdom I've ever learnt. And am still learning. Churchill captured it beautifully.

"Life can either be accepted or changed. If it is not accepted, it must be changed. If it cannot be changed, then it must be accepted."

WINSTON CHURCHILL, STATESMAN, SOLDIER AND WRITER, FORMER UK PRIME MINISTER

Actionable advice

Accepting how things are doesn't mean that you have to *like* them. Often, you won't like the situation you find yourself in. It simply means that you learn to stop *fighting* it and surrender.

> "*Surrender means wisely accommodating ourselves to what is beyond our control.*"
> **SYLVIA BOORSTEIN, AUTHOR, PSYCHOTHERAPIST AND BUDDHIST TEACHER**

Sometimes your ability to influence events is severely limited. Being stuck on a mezzanine level between not changing and not accepting is a painful and stressful place to be. So if you can't change it, *do your absolute level best* to accept it. No matter how hard that is.

> "*You may not control all the events that happen to you, but you can decide not to be reduced by them.*"
> **MAYA ANGELOU, MEMOIRIST, POET AND CIVIL RIGHTS ACTIVIST**

This is also closely linked to how you respond or react to a "negative" situation. Imagine two people facing the same "bad" situation. One can choose to go into drama. Catastrophising. Focusing on the negative. Seeing another future disaster as a result. The other can see it as an opportunity to do something unexpected or different. Depends on your mindset. Fixed mindset or growth mindset? Optimist or pessimist? So when things get tough, you can either look at it as an excellent opportunity to practise being gritty, or find your sense of humour – or you can dive under the duvet and have a hissy fit.

> *"When we are no longer able to change a situation, we are challenged to change ourselves."*
> **VIKTOR E. FRANKL, PSYCHIATRIST AND HOLOCAUST SURVIVOR**

So *how we perceive* events that happen to us is important. In Buddhism, there's a wonderful thing called the Parable of the Two Arrows. Imagine you're walking in the woods and you get hit by an arrow. SFB. (That's Shit Fuck Bollocks, by the way… which I reserve for very bad situations. Getting hit by an arrow is definitely one of those.) The Buddha describes the first arrow as the physical pain. Ouch. You can't do much about that. The second arrow however, is what your *mind* does. It starts thinking about the worst scenario. It catastrophises. Buddha says, "Be warned of the second arrow." The second arrow is what we call suffering. So, there's a difference between pain and suffering. *Pain is inevitable but the suffering is something we create in our minds. We just don't realise we're doing it.* There's a sense of resistance to it because we're not accepting the reality of a situation. We're not allowing it to be there. So we add suffering on top of the pain. Double whammy. The wisdom from this is that the pain is inevitable but the level of suffering is actually optional. This is a big one to wrap your head round. It sounds tough and unrealistic. Of course you're going to suffer if a loved one dies. But maybe try to take this wisdom into a slightly less horrible situation and just understand how you're reacting or overreacting?

> *"Suffering usually relates to wanting things to be different from the way they are."*
> **ALLAN LOKOS, FOUNDER AND GUIDING TEACHER, COMMUNITY MEDITATION CENTRE, NYC**

Think about the last time something "bad" happened to you – it could be something really small, an everyday situation. How did you handle it? Did you accept the situation or did you fight it? Did you step into your drama queen? Did you make it worse by your reaction?

> *"Pain is the feeling. Suffering is the effect the pain inflicts. If one can endure pain, one can live without suffering. If one can withstand pain, one can withstand anything. If one can learn to control pain, one can learn to control oneself."*
> **JAMES FREY, AUTHOR, MY FRIEND LEONARD**

ACTION/CONSIDERATION

Can you think of a situation in your life that you're struggling to accept right now?

What are you fighting?

*Generally, when something painful happens to you,
how do you deal with it?*

*Do you have any tendencies to overdramatise things?
Or do you underplay situations?*

*Can you strip out the part that you have some control
over and the part that you can't control?*

PEARL 32

....

Exercise courage regularly

> *"Do something that scares you every day."*
> **ELEANOR ROOSEVELT, DIPLOMAT, POLITICAL**
> **ACTIVIST AND FORMER FIRST LADY OF THE US**

Every day might be a *little* unrealistic but I definitely think Eleanor was on to something here. Firstly, we understand that doing stuff regularly just works. And if you want to be the best version of you, the brutal truth of it, is that from time to time you'll need to take some courageous decisions. Have some uncomfortable conversations. Or take a leap of faith. Whatever it is, you're going to need to be brave and put your big-girl pants on. My suggestion is that you view courage like a muscle which needs regular exercise. Otherwise it becomes weak, and then *you* become weak.

> *"Life begins at the end of your comfort zone."*
> **UNKNOWN**

Actionable advice

To help build your courage muscle, there are a couple of things to bear in mind. Firstly, how do you view failure? What is your mindset around learning? And what is your level of resilience or grit? It's much easier to be courageous if you *know* you can withstand the consequences of it all going pear-shaped. Uncomfortable, yes. But bearable. You'll be OK. Courage and grit go hand in hand.

"Fear is a reaction. Courage is a decision."
WINSTON CHURCHILL, STATESMAN, SOLDIER AND WRITER, FORMER UK PRIME MINISTER

One way of building adaptability, courage and resilience is gentle exposure. Gradually exposing yourself to something "scary" or difficult and then working through what happens on the other side. You'll experience a sense of exhilaration when you make a leap into the unknown. You'll feel alive with a sense of achievement. When you start to feel comfortable with being uncomfortable you know you're making real strides in your growth journey. And it doesn't have to be throwing yourself off a cliff or skydiving. Start small. Just exercise your courage muscle more often.

"Change is inevitable. Growth is optional."
JOHN C. MAXWELL, AUTHOR, SPEAKER AND PASTOR

I used to have a real problem with spiders. On one occasion, I had to use my neighbour's loo as there was a huge spider in my bathroom. I simply couldn't muster the courage to go in there and I only had one loo in that cottage. So I went to see a friend of mine who's a hypnotherapist and we had a little chat with my subconscious.

Nowadays, I exercise my courage muscle whenever I see a spider. I just look at it for a moment. I don't panic, so I don't engage my flight or fight trigger. I breathe and pause and I look at it. Then I go and get my spider catcher and I carefully escort it off the premises, trying not to harm it. I *always* feel a huge sense of pride and empowerment after I've done this as I remember how crippling it used to be. Many years ago, I did an NLP training with Paul McKenna in London. After a few days of working on hypnotic techniques, we got the "opportunity" to get intimately acquainted with either a spider or a snake. So I had Octavia sit on my hand for a moment or two. Octavia was a large brown furry tarantula, so that was a big deal for me, let me tell you. It's the difficult stuff that makes you grow as a person. If I get wobbly when I see a house spider, I gently remind myself that I had the mother of all arachnids sitting on my hand for a while. So I can deal with this much smaller relative who finds itself in my bath with no sweat whatsoever!

It's very easy to get overwhelmed when you take on a new project or try out new behaviours, particularly if they're pushing you out of your comfort zone. So the question I

always want you to ask yourself is, "what baby step can I take to start me off?" What's an achievable first small step that will get you on your way? And that's all you need to start.

> *"The journey of a thousand miles begins with a single step."*
> **LAO TZU, ANCIENT PHILOSOPHER**

Some of the teachings of Buddhism focus on change. Impermanence is a big deal for Buddhists. The fact that everything changes is the basic truth for all existence. And you know this. Nothing ever really stays the same, even from one moment to the next. So if you know you're uncomfortable with change, life is going to be a little challenging. Which you might want to explore. It can take courage to change.

One way to grow more comfortable with change, is to learn to adapt yourself to external shifts. Just like building courage, it's about increased exposure. You can either do this by putting yourself into situations where there's lots of change OR by *choosing* to implement change in your daily life. The only way to make yourself more adaptable is to consciously *decide to flex* as often as you can. I'm not suggesting a wholesale change of everything in your life tomorrow. Although if you're cool with that, go for it! It's more about consciously choosing to take a more flexible approach. To see another view. If the branches of a tree aren't flexible, they'll snap in a storm. If they bend with the storm, they'll survive. Flexibility is an important attribute to master in today's constantly fast-changing world.

ACTION/CONSIDERATION

Where in your life could you be more courageous?

Is there anything coming up for you that seems like an immense project or task?

What's the first baby step you could take to kick you off?

How flexible do you think you are?

If you find change difficult, what small alterations can you make to your routine to start building flexibility?

PEARL 33

·····························

Understand the danger of attachment

> *"Make deep connections, not deep attachments."*
> **YUNG PUEBLO, AUTHOR**

A big blocker to happiness and source of dissatisfaction, anxiety and stress, particularly in the West, is our deep *attachment* to stuff. Outcomes, expectations and of course, possessions. And when outcomes or expectations aren't met, we can suffer. We suffer because we are *so* attached to them. It *has* to be this way. It *has* to be that way. It *has* to be right. *I* have to be right. And when you're unable to control events, this is a complete waste of your energy. And it's pretty stressful. Most of the problems people have in the world and the stuff that therapists spend their lives dealing with, have their roots in our attachments.

There are an awful lot of people in this world who are so attached to their positions, their ideals, views and opinions that they've become completely intolerant to other people's views and opinions. You can see how dangerous this level of attachment is. It becomes dogmatic and extremely harmful to society. The amount of intolerance and lack of understanding of another's point of view in both the real world and on social media is one of our biggest problems. Being conscious of your attachments is really important, so you stay balanced and compassionate.

Actionable advice

In Buddhism they talk about something called *"non-attachment"*. Non-attachment is the ability to *not be emotionally attached* to things or events that control you or affect you in a way that's not good for you. Now this doesn't mean you're *"detached"* from an outcome, situation or expectation. Being detached implies you're indifferent and don't give a shit, which isn't what we're talking about here. Non-attachment is about creating a sense of calm and distance from a situation. So the situation still exists, it's just that you're not so wholly emotionally bound up in it and feeling angst about it. Military doctors who are constantly dealing with the most dire of human catastrophes have to either learn this or naturally have an element of non-attachment to be able to do their jobs.

Possessions, particularly expensive status symbols, can start to *define* you if you're not careful. When I got engaged, I chose a very beautiful ring or as I sometimes say, *it* chose me. It was winking at me from the black velvet baize tray. It's a fuck-off massive bright-blue aquamarine surrounded by a whole cluster of diamonds. A real showstopper. And of course I expressed myself expansively and deliberately, wafting my left hand around so it was in full sight at all times. I'd get comments from men as well as women. People who worked in banks, post offices, London Underground staff, shop assistants, waitresses. And then one day I had a bit of an aha moment. I realised I didn't want to be defined by my ring anymore. I didn't want *that* to be what people saw. I wear my ring occasionally these days. I'm much more conscious of what it represents and my relationship with it. I guess I've just become a little less emotionally attached to it, more *"non-attached"*.

And sometimes, the more expensive the things you buy, the more stressful and expensive it can be to protect them. The wisdom here is to understand *why* you're buying a handbag, a watch, a ring, a car or any other status symbol. Is it the quality of their beauty, their design and engineering? Just ask yourself what's your *intention* when you buy these things? Is it for you or is it for show? Is it to tell the world "you've arrived" because you can afford a Prada handbag? That can be a tough one to admit to yourself. How important is the status? How attached are you? I'm not saying don't aspire to buy nice things, but just be careful about how *dependent* you become. Do you really want to be identified by a handbag or a pair of shoes?

Another way that attachment can trip you up is by your getting totally fixated on *one particular course of action, route or outcome*. You've got a firm idea in your head of the way you think things *should* be or *should* work out according to you. You'll push and push in order to make it happen. Even if things are constantly getting in the way and conspiring against you. Has that ever happened to you? What I've found over the years is that sometimes you need to take note of what's going on and just accept the way things are. Sometimes you need to let go of the pushing and the effort and embrace acceptance. Get off your quest to make things happen when sometimes they're clearly *not* going to happen. Or not going to happen in your chosen time frame! I call it *pushing water uphill* and the Maasai tribe have a very clear view on it.

> *"You cannot force water up a hill."*
> **MAASAI PROVERB**

ACTION/CONSIDERATION

What possessions, outcomes or expectations are you strongly attached to?

When was the last time you clung on to an outcome even though it was obvious it wasn't going to happen (at least not in your desired time frame?)

PEARL 34

....

Enjoy the journey

> *"It is good to have an end to journey toward; but it is the journey that matters, in the end."*
> **URSULA K. LE GUIN, AUTHOR**

Today's society is a little obsessed with the endgame. The destination. Setting goals and achieving objectives. But it's equally important for you to just appreciate the pleasure of *enjoying the journey*. Whatever that is.

> *"A good traveller has no fixed plans and is not intent on arriving."*
> **LAO TZU, ANCIENT PHILOSOPHER**

You wouldn't ask a child why they're playing in the sea. They're not doing it to achieve an objective. They're doing it because they can and it's bloody good fun. So as an adult, don't feel pressured to have a goal or endgame in mind all the time. Just having fun is an endgame in itself. Please never forget that.

162

My whole life, I'd always wanted to make candles but just never got round to it. Lockdown gave me the perfect opportunity. I ordered a set of "make your own" from a lovely company called True Grace and I was off! I enjoyed the process so much I started selling them. I built a website, created a market stall and sold my convertible so I could buy a 4x4 with a ginormous boot. And I did that for a couple of years. And when I felt like I didn't want to do it anymore, I stopped. I never wanted to be Jo Malone. It was a hobby. A bit of a side hustle. Everyone kept asking me where I was going to "take the business" or what was next. Frankly, I had no idea. I was just doing it because I enjoyed it. And when I found standing on a freezing market stall in the dark with five layers on a little tiresome, I stopped doing it. In fact, the catalyst was when I felt it was *distracting me from my own North Star*. So I called a halt. Happily and willingly. I sold the business on eBay, which was wonderfully unexpected. Then I could focus on my priority project at the time.

> *"We think that accomplishing things will complete us, when it is experiencing life that will."*
> **MARK NEPO, POET AND SPIRITUAL ADVISER**

Actionable advice

Whether it's a creative process, a sport or a hobby, you don't have to do anything with it. Just enjoy doing it. There doesn't always need to be an objective. While it *is* important to have a North Star and a sense of direction, it's also important to enjoy the process. So please never be afraid to just do stuff for the hell of it.

And in the spirit of moving away from goal-orientated New Year's resolutions, how about choosing a ***word*** for next year instead? A word which embodies a quality? It could be something like balance, courage or abundance… one word that you can apply to lots of areas of your life. "Courage" could mean you go out of your comfort zone more often, you take more risks, you choose not to take the easy option. Pushing yourself just a little more.

It could be a mantra. "Quality over quantity." That could apply to everything from your food shopping to your clothes choices to your friends. It's more relaxed and fluid than a resolution or goal. *"Lose a stone"* is very goal-orientated. *"Choose healthier options"* is a way of life which could apply not only to your shopping basket but getting out in nature more or choosing not to have that third glass of wine!

ACTION/CONSIDERATION

Do you feel pressured to achieve goals and objectives to the detriment of enjoying the journey?

Which aspects of your life or which activities could

you do just for the hell of it without having to achieve an outcome?

If you were going to choose a word or mantra to live your life by for the next 12 months, what could that be?

Which areas of your life could you immediately apply it to?

PEARL 35

....

Disarm your perfectionist

> *"...a high-end haute couture version of fear..."*
> ***ELIZABETH GILBERT, AUTHOR,*** BIG MAGIC

We talked earlier about Resistance sometimes popping up as Perfectionism. We need to talk about "the Perfectionist" because I see her a lot in my work, as well as in myself from time to time. I even hear it as a badge of honour from some of my clients. "The thing is… you know… I'm a bit of a perfectionist." There's a tinge of pride in that statement. Now, don't get me wrong, it's great to aim high. I'm not suggesting you get sloppy with your work, but tying yourself up in knots in the everyday tasks is something else entirely. Or not even *starting* something because you don't think it will ever be good enough is just not smart and a waste of your talents.

There are two areas of my life where this shows up most. Singing and yoga. The other day in my yoga class, we were doing balancing poses. Now, if you practise yoga, you'll know that some days your balance is good. And some days it just sucks. For any number of reasons. It's the mind that usually gets in the way. For me, it's about knowing that I'm pretty good at something and I *ought* to be able to do it better than I'm currently doing it. I *should* be able to do a perfect tree pose with no problem. But instead, there I am at the front of the class wobbling around like a novice, getting very cross with myself. Then I smile as I recognise what's going on. "Just let it go." Let go of the *"I ought to be able to do this", "I can usually do this", "I'm good at this", "why is this happening, this is so frustrating?"* bullshit and just relax and let it *flow*. In fact, one answer to this conundrum is having fun with it. I think the ego is a serious critter and one way of disarming it is with humour.

> *"There are plenty of difficult obstacles in your path.*
> *Don't allow yourself to become one of them."*
> **RALPH MARSTON, AUTHOR AND PUBLISHER,**
> **THE DAILY MOTIVATOR**

When I allowed my sense of humour to enter the frame and I accepted that I was a wobbly tree that night and that was the way it was, I felt a whole load better. My mind and my ego were just getting in the way. So sometimes you need to let things just be and simply flow with what is. Accept and move on. Stop trying to control what you sometimes *can't* control. Remember that Serenity Prayer.

The same happened the other day in a singing lesson. We were practising for an upcoming concert and I was trying to sing Ella Fitzgerald's 'The Lady is a Tramp'. I had to stop twice. I felt tight and tense. I wasn't in the flow at all. My singing teacher who I've known for years, stopped the music. "You're overthinking it again. Let go of it being perfect. Just try and not give so much of a fuck." That's exactly what I needed to hear. **_Don't give so much of a fuck._** Just have fun and entertain the audience, that's what matters. Getting every note perfect was screwing me over. I relaxed, decided to have fun with it and hey presto, it was better immediately.

Actionable advice

Remember you have a duty to share your gifts with the world. Being a perfectionist can really screw that up. Very often, we're our own worst enemy and get in our own way. I've done it myself so many times and I see others doing it without even realising. At work, you can always manage other people's expectations when it comes to deadlines. Sometimes it's better to get it done to 80% to meet a deadline, rather than to 100% and be late.

Pursuing perfection is like chasing a rainbow, or the horizon. It's a mythical destination that we're striving for which mostly doesn't exist. And I use the word *strive* deliberately as it implies angst and hardship, like pushing water uphill. And back to the singing example. If you look at it in energetic terms, trying to deliver a perfect rendition was tightening and tensing my energy and that was affecting my voice. Once I let go of *striving*, my energy changed to a more relaxed, flowy, fun vibe and my voice was better and stronger.

Have a go at *"seeking excellence"* rather than *"striving for perfection"*. Excellence is more of an *attitude* rather than a destination. It allows for flexibility and embraces failure as a necessary part of the process of seeking. It's more forgiving and in the word "seek" there's a sense of curiosity rather than failure. Why didn't that work? That's interesting. What happened? How could you do that differently next time? It's also about prioritising progress over perfection. Have a go at adopting the "done is better than perfect" attitude. Get stuff done and out. Then move on to the next thing. Perfectionism is rigid, inflexible and controlling and will often result in stress because it consumes so much of your time and energy.

ACTION/CONSIDERATION

If you have a perfectionist, where does she tend to show up in your life?

How does it play out? What happens?

How can she cause you problems?

Where in your life could you start to ease back on always having to get it to 100%?

What would you have to do differently?

PEARL 36

....

Understand the imposter

> *"I still have a little impostor syndrome... It doesn't go away, that feeling that you shouldn't take me that seriously. What do I know? I share that with you because we all have doubts in our abilities, about our power and what that power is."*
> **MICHELLE OBAMA, ATTORNEY, AUTHOR AND FORMER FIRST LADY OF THE US**

If I had a quid for every client who's told me they suffer from Imposter Syndrome, I'd be as rich as Elon. If you get the odd visit from the Imposter too, let's have a look at what's going on.

Imposter Syndrome is rooted in the belief that somehow everyone else is more capable than you. That you're not worthy of being in their "club". That you don't deserve to be there. Back to comparison. You're constantly comparing yourself to others and coming off worse. You're comparing your angst-ridden inner world where you know all the messy reality to someone else's carefully curated outer world. But do you really think you're alone in this? Do you really think everyone else has got life totally sussed and doesn't have all these self-doubts? Of course not. What I would say is that some people are better at handling the outer façade than others. And clearly some people get the knock on the door from the Imposter, but they just refuse to open it.

Most of us have a visit from the Imposter from time to time. I was looking at some research* the other day, which showed that 75% of women have reported suffering from Imposter Syndrome at some point in their careers. That's a ridiculously large number, so what the hell's going on?

Sometimes it goes back to those messages you've been fed as a child. By your parents and teachers. Some schools instil in their pupils a sense of superiority and super confidence. Our society is still a factor in the way it discriminates. Either that you *absolutely* have a right to be at the top table *or* that you don't. And so those who believe they have a right to be there will have a different inner dialogue. And maybe no inner critic giving them a hard time. Maybe they don't constantly compare themselves to others? Maybe their resilience is stronger? Their relationship to failure may be healthier? Maybe they've cultivated a different relationship with themselves? Or maybe they've got skin like a rhino and absolutely zero self-awareness? And this outward layer of arrogance would never allow the Imposter to penetrate. I can think of a few politicians like that…

Actionable advice

Everyone deals with the feelings of Imposter Syndrome slightly differently, but there are a few things for you to think about. Occasionally, the feeling of being an Imposter is actually rooted in something real and logical. It may be that you *do* need some extra training, coaching or support to be better at your job. That's totally logical. So ask for it. Remember, you need to take responsibility for your own personal development.

But, if you have a sense that your feelings of Imposter Syndrome are ***totally illogical*** when you rationalise the situation, pay attention to your inner critic. Listen to what it's saying. Then comfort and reassure it. The adult you needs to reassure the scared part of yourself. The Imposter can be linked to that primeval part of the brain that wants to protect you, keep you small and stop you making an arse of yourself. Or it goes back to the disempowering beliefs that you've sucked up as a child without any filters. That you're not worthy. That you don't belong. Because of your gender, sexuality, colour of your skin, background. Whatever. Giving yourself your own personal validation and reaffirming all the good stuff you do and have done is a good start. Do this, rather than focusing on the negative chat from the inner critic who's trying to sabotage you to keep you safe. It's also about acknowledging your strengths, talents and abilities on a regular basis. This is really empowering, yet few people do it. We'll talk about Personal Brand later because that's really going to help you connect with your strengths and superpowers, something that most people struggle with. It's about validating *to yourself* that you're as smart, capable, experienced and worthy as everyone else in "the room".

The Imposter will often turn up when you find yourself about to leap into a growth situation. It's a form of Resistance – which we know is just fear. A promotion is a classic one. "I'm not up to it", "What if I can't handle it?", "What will they think of me?", "I'm not in their league". Well, somebody obviously thought you were, otherwise they wouldn't have promoted you.

If you want to make yourself even more resilient against the Imposter, there's something else you can play with. If you can reframe your *relationship with failure*, you remove a lot of the Imposter's ammunition. If you start to see failing as learning, you become *way* more bulletproof. And no one likes failing but if you can shift your mindset to understanding what happened and learn from it, rather than falling apart, you'll be in much better shape. Forgive and accept yourself when things go wrong. And if you can choose to take notice of the self-supporting voice rather than the harsh, judging critic, that's real growth. Try giving yourself a hug when you screw up rather than being tough and calling yourself an idiot.

And sometimes it's about your ability to be vulnerable and to accept you *don't* have all the answers. No-one does. You're big enough not to pretend. You're big enough to be real. There's huge power in that. Just *own* it. It doesn't mean you don't deserve to be at the top table. It doesn't mean that you don't deserve to be in the room. It just means you're big enough to know your limitations. Saying "I don't know" is, counterintuitively, rather powerful.

ACTION/CONSIDERATION

Are there any areas of your life where you feel you don't belong or where you feel inferior to others?

Can you put your finger on what's causing that?

What are the beliefs or fears?

Are you able to strip out the rational from the irrational?

How could you respond differently to the Imposter if she comes knocking?

PEARL 37

....

Turn failure to your advantage

> *"Our greatest glory is not in never falling,*
> *but in rising every time we fall."*
> **CONFUCIUS, PHILOSOPHER**

There are a few certainties in this life. At some point, you'll die. If you drive, you'll get cut up by a white-van man. And you'll never be rid of the taxman. Take it from me. Oh yes – and you'll fail. Not only will you fail, you will fail again and again. And again. At something. We all fail. It's part of being human. And you know what? You *need* to fail. As utterly shitty as it might feel at the time, it's necessary. Why? Because if you can learn to fail *well*, that, my lovely, is extremely powerful.

Is she really serious?
Yep. Failure is an essential part of life.

I was talking to a young client of mine recently. She's 27 and doing well. She went for an interview for an internal promotion and didn't get the job. For a week she went into meltdown, had a few epic hissy fits and licked her wounds.

Then the magic happened.

The wise, adult, rational part of her took control of the scared, emotional part. She picked herself up, made a plan and determined that for the next year her sole focus was going to be doing whatever it took to get the job next time it came up. She put all her energies into researching what was needed. She started to act "as if" she was doing the new role. She had a powerful sense of her North Star and put everything she could into nailing the interview next time round. It paid off. She got promoted.

She chose to be resilient. It would have been so easy for her to think, "fuck it, they don't appreciate me, I'm off." But instead, she turned her energy into a passion and got fired up. She told me how wonderful that failure was. *"It put a bomb under my arse."* She turned failure to her advantage.

Thirty years ago when I started my coaching business, I got the opportunity to present my wares to a training and coaching outsourcing business. This company ran a lot of programmes for the likes of Virgin and Boots, so being "on their books" would have been a lucrative gig for someone starting out. I was psyched. I travelled all the way from London to Leicester on what felt like the slowest train on the planet and then waited to be called in. I walked into a huge room with possibly the largest (and most intimidating) oval table I'd ever seen, which was polished to within an inch of its life. There were a few people dotted round said table. We said our hellos and then they asked me to showcase my stuff.

Showcase my stuff? That wasn't what I was expecting. Fuck. I thought I was going to chat to a few people about what I did, how I worked and who I worked for. They clearly wanted me to run a dummy training session. They kept asking me to *show* them how I worked, and I kept *telling* them how I worked. This went on for what seemed like an eternity until they finally thanked me for my time and showed me to the door. Without doubt, it was one of the most humiliating experiences of my entire life. It was also one of the biggest misunderstandings of a brief and a mismatch of expectations I'd ever made. And to make it even worse, the introduction had come through an old contact who'd recommended me! It couldn't have got more embarrassing. Needless to say, that was the last I ever heard of him! I just can't imagine what the feedback must have been; I still cringe when I think about it today. But I learned an incredibly powerful lesson.

Preparation, preparation, preparation.

Understand the brief. Clarify the brief. Ask if you need to. Don't ever think you can wing it. You can't.

Actionable advice

Whether falling or failing, however you want to frame it, you need to emerge from this dense, cringe-inducing fog with a clear understanding of what went wrong and what you need to do differently. Gritty and resilient people aren't afraid to fail. Why? Because they know failure is a learning process and not a life-defining event that will forever consign them to the dark recesses of being a loser.

There are hugely important and valuable lessons to be learned in defeat. As disappointing and painful (ghastly flashback to the polished oval table) as it may be, you need to ask yourself, how can I turn this around and make it work for me? And you know, there will be times when there's absolutely bugger all you could have done differently. It was entirely out of your control. So accept it and move on. And that's a valuable lesson in itself.

In recent years, there seems to have been a trend towards protecting our youngsters from failing. Which, in my humble opinion, is utterly barking. Parents and teachers who wrap children in cotton wool and protect them from failing, or being disappointed, are doing those kids a massive disservice. By doing this early on, they're setting our youngsters up to be fragile and flaky without any resilience. By removing competition in sports or encouraging the mantra that "everyone's a winner", they're essentially sheltering them from reality. Not everyone *is* a winner. Failure and disappointment are just as much a part of life as success and happiness. We live in a competitive world, whether it's education, sports or the workplace.

You need to be able to embrace the pain of a loss rather than avoiding it. And if you do lose, please do it with grace (and with a dogged commitment to address what you could do differently). Learning to lose gracefully is important in life. I was playing a mixed doubles tennis match the other day and we beat our opponents in straight sets. We were just better than they were. But the man was really pissed off that he lost. When we shook hands, he couldn't even look at me. A man in his fifties sulking because he lost. Wasn't a great look.

If you have those Perfectionist tendencies we talked about earlier, failure is going to be your nemesis. The thing you try to avoid at all costs. So, you've got to reframe failure and start acknowledging that your inner perfectionist is actually doing you a huge disservice. Perfectionism will cut you off from the possibility of success, creativity and growth quicker than you can say the words, "I can't possibly fail".

> *"There is no innovation and creativity without failure. Period."*
> **BRENÉ BROWN, PROFESSOR, RESEARCHER AND AUTHOR**

If you invest so much of your time and energy in making sure absolutely nothing could go wrong, it will suck the living breath out of you. And it will stop you participating fully in life because you're afraid you might not be brilliant at everything so you never even start. Remember when we talked about seeking excellence rather than striving for perfection? By embracing the idea of seeing failing as a learning mechanism, you'll find it easier to refine, review and tweak and then come up with another plan. Failure is 100% a creative learning process. Reframing your ideas around failure is going to be a game changer. Perfectionists always feel rejection deeply and it's often accompanied by "it's not fair" (the martyr might make a sweeping entrance here just to jazz things up a little). Swiftly followed by "Fuck it, I give up" and possibly a justification: "It was a crap idea/project/job anyway." Building the habit of always asking, "What did I learn, now let's try that again" is a fabulous place to be. Trust me, it will set you free.

Before we move on, let's talk about our old friend, the Inner Critic. How does *she* sound when you screw up? "You're such a muppet, why did you do that?" "Oh God, that's so *typical* of you." "I *knew* you wouldn't be able to pull it off…why did you even try? Now everyone thinks you're stupid."

Blah, blah, blah.

Your inner critic just thrives on a good, juicy failure. Remember – it's trying to protect you from doing anything that's going to make you grow. So when you fail, your inner critic will leap up and down telling you, "I told you so. Why didn't you listen to me?" And that narrative can be pretty damning as well as paralysing. You need to rewrite the script on that one to be kinder and more compassionate to yourself in defeat. Personally, I find humour useful to disarm the situation and lighten the tone a little. Make it less serious and see it for what it is. It's a cliché but it isn't the end of the world. You will rebound and live another day. Give yourself a massive hug and move on.

> *"Success consists of going from failure to*
> *failure without loss of enthusiasm."*
> **WINSTON CHURCHILL, STATESMAN, SOLDIER**
> **AND WRITER, FORMER UK PRIME MINISTER**

Imagine if Edison had stopped trying the first time he failed. No light-bulb moments for any of us. In fact, he tried over 10,000 different ways to make a light bulb before he hit on the right formula. He famously said, "I haven't failed, I just found 10,000 ways that didn't work." He also said, "Opportunity is missed by most people because it's dressed in overalls and looks like work." If you're failing well – it's work. So roll your sleeves up and get stuck into a plan of action.

I know failure is deeply unpleasant. If you were the reason your company lost a pitch worth millions of pounds because you tanked, of course that's going to suck beyond belief. But when you're done feeling sorry for yourself and feeling guilty, you need to revisit what happened and ask yourself why.

Action *always* helps. Bringing some positive energy to the situation is also useful. Put plans in place to ensure you don't make the same mistake twice. Edison's notebooks are legendary. He made notes of every attempt so he wouldn't repeat something that hadn't worked.

Maybe seek some advice, particularly from the people who may have been involved in the failure (this can be uncomfortable but it's probably going to be one of the most useful conversations you'll ever have). Let them see that you're owning it, taking responsibility and getting something positive out of the experience. That in itself will do you a lot of good in terms of how people perceive you. If you can fail well, it shows grit and maturity.

OK, now there's a caveat to all of this. I'm very conscious that you need to protect your mental health. Of course you do. Everyone does. Don't put yourself in situations that are genuinely detrimental to your well-being. But ask yourself honestly, are you opting out of situations simply because they're just a bit too tough or too difficult? If the answer to that is yes then you're missing out on a whole load of living and growth. You're keeping yourself small. You'll feel much better about yourself if you try your best to do something rather than just completely opting out. Regret is not trying. "Let me have a go" will never be bad for your mental health.

Of course, there's another reason you need to embrace failure. Becoming more accepting and forgiving of your own frailties, weaknesses and vulnerabilities will help you be more tolerant of those traits in others. You become more compassionate and that's really important. Right now, more than ever, the world needs you to be more compassionate to others.

Building your resilience is one of the most important things you can do for your personal and professional growth. As well as the tools we've already discussed, there are some basic things to get in place which will positively affect your levels of resilience. Good physical health plays a big part in helping you to become more resilient in the face of stress, change and failure. Good diet, rest, good sleep, minimal intake of addictive stuff will all help you to be more robust when the shit hits the fan. We've talked about being present and using mindfulness as a stress buster. As stress happens in your body, practising any kind of body awareness like Pilates, yoga or t'ai chi can only be beneficial. You can also practise breathing properly.

> *"Conscious breathing is the best antidote to stress, anxiety and depression."*
> **AMIT RAY, AUTHOR AND SPIRITUAL MASTER**

When you get stressed, you may find yourself taking quick, shallow breaths which activates your fight or flight instincts. Try breathing through your nose deep into your belly, and instead you'll activate your calming, restoring, digestion-boosting parasympathetic nervous system. Much better.

The other thing that's clearly going to help you when times are tough is the support network of your family and friends. Don't be afraid to reach out for some help and comfort from those who know you well and love you.

ACTION/CONSIDERATION

When did you last fail at something?
(It could be something really small.)

What was your first reaction?

What emotions and thoughts came up?

How did you deal with it?

What can you change to build your resilience?

PEARL 38

....

Know when to cut your losses

> *"A hallmark of wisdom is knowing when to grit and when to quit."*
> **ADAM GRANT, AMERICAN AUTHOR AND PROFESSOR**

By far the best way to describe this Pearl of Wisdom is to give you a very recent example of something that happened to me in Miami of all places. It's a useful one because it can eliminate stress. And to me, anything that reduces stress is worth knowing. This is about the importance of being able to exit a situation when you think it's going badly wrong.

I'd left my luggage at the same hotel where I'd stayed for two nights before joining my jazz cruise. When the cruise was over, the rather charming young concierge assured me I could leave my bags with him while I toured Miami on the bus before heading off for my evening flight to London.

So, after getting off the Big Red Bus tour (highly recommended if you ever find yourself in Miami with a few hours to kill), I hailed a yellow cab. First big mistake. Rookie error. Note to self – never do that again.

I'd hailed a yellow cab with a taxi driver who had limited English and apparently an even more limited knowledge of the streets of Miami. Which, by the way, is based on a grid system which should supposedly make it easier to navigate. His cab was also making the kinds of noises you'd expect to hear if bits of it were about to drop off. The deal I'd struck with his "boss" was: drop me at the hotel, wait two minutes for me to grab my bags and then head off to the airport. Nice fare for him. Minimal hassle for me. Or so I thought.

As we got within a few blocks of the hotel, the driver handed me his phone to try to work out the last part of the journey as he'd got no idea where he was going. I'd given him the address but he wasn't even using his phone or Google Maps to navigate his way round. I handed the phone back to him, politely reminding him that *I was the tourist* and I was paying *him* to get me to the hotel. This was met with mild abuse and mutterings about how I was putting him under pressure and stressing him out. I finally recognised where we were and got us back to the hotel.

It was at that moment that I made the crucial decision to *cut my losses*. I didn't want this guy trying to get me to the airport to catch my flight to London. No way, José. I looked at the meter. Seven dollars and fifty cents. So I handed him a ten-dollar bill, said, "Thank you, but I was getting out," This was followed by more abuse. Totally fine. I was glad to be out of the cab before the bumper fell off.

I asked my friendly concierge to order me a taxi. Within ten minutes a large, shiny, black, air-conditioned people-carrier arrived, complete with a compartment full of bottles of iced water and a driver who loved British music from the sixties. So I arrived stress-free at Miami International Airport, having been treated to Gerry & The Pacemakers and The Beatles.

Result.

Actionable advice

So, what could have been the alternative if I hadn't made that decision? Who knows, but I suspect it would have been more stressful. Even if my original driver did know the way to the airport, I still wasn't convinced that part of his cab wasn't going to fall off.

It takes courage to exit situations and relationships. It's far easier and more comfortable to stay with the way things are rather than pivot. But you need to be able to see ahead at what *could* happen if you continue down your chosen path. Mine was a rather minor example but it could apply to far more consequential situations, relationships or sets of circumstances. And you need to trust your instincts. If something doesn't feel right and you don't like the look of what you're seeing ahead, don't stick with it because you "feel bad". It's no good saying, "Oh, it'll be fine". Because if your intuition is nagging you, there's a very good chance it won't be fine. You'll feel a lot worse if you end up in a stressful situation because you didn't cut your losses.

ACTION/CONSIDERATION

Have you ever been in a situation where you just stayed too long?

Can you put your finger on why?

At what point could you have cut your losses?

What could you say to yourself to stop this happening again in the future?

PEARL 39

Practise "can" rather than "have to"

> *"Do things when you can, not when you have to."*
> **SASSY GODMOTHER, AUTHOR, SPEAKER AND SPIRITUAL ADVENTURER**

This little Pearl of Wisdom has been with me for years. I picked it up from a friend who'd been on a sailing course. It was the mantra they used on the boat. Don't wait until you're in the middle of rough weather to fix the ropes or clear the decks when it's clearly too late. I used it a lot when I was looking after my parents. Forward thinking. Contingency planning. Being one step ahead. Whatever you want to call it. It makes life a hell of a lot less stressful.

Both my parents had dementia, which sadly, mostly only goes in one direction, so I knew I had to future-proof their house, stage by stage, to accommodate their declining state. This meant anything from getting grab rails fitted, to special loo seats, to creating a walk-in wet room or putting signs up on cupboards and doors to remind them where things were. I became the Mistress of *Do It When You Can, Not When You Have To* in order to accommodate their needs. This is about getting things in place when you have the luxury of time. I did the same thing when I knew they'd need to go into a care home. The good homes had waiting lists, so, well in advance, I went and looked round a number of them. I drew up a shortlist and got my name down for my top choices. And when the time came for them to move into their respective care homes, I'd ensured they both had the best care possible. And I have to say, that's something I'm extremely proud of to this day.

Actionable advice

You're more likely to make good, measured, informed decisions when you're not stressed, when you're not under time pressure and circumstances are closing in on you. You don't have to end up with what's left if you just take action a bit sooner. Why settle for second best when you can have your first choice?

Of course it's tempting to put things off. Particularly if it involves making difficult and uncomfortable decisions. Believe me, putting a parent in a care home is right up there. I felt like I was playing God with my parents' lives. So doing the right thing had never been so important. Being courageous to face into something you can see on the horizon and taking early action could save you a lot of stress down the line. We know procrastination can be a form of Resistance, which is just the fear of being uncomfortable. Why do you put anything off? Because something's making you feel uneasy and you'd rather stay where you are. Just like learning to cut your losses, doing nothing is the easy way out. You need to be able to recognise our old friend Resistance when it rears its ugly head.

ACTION/CONSIDERATION

Looking at the foreseeable future, what situations or circumstances are coming your way?

What can you do NOW to prepare?

Are there any situations which are particularly difficult or challenging?

Is there any resistance popping up?

How is that manisfesting itself?

PEARL 40

Make peace with discomfort

> *"Discomfort is the price of admission for a meaningful life."*
> **DR SUSAN DAVID, PSYCHOLOGIST**

This is a biggie. And a tricky one. When you suffer emotionally or endure physical pain, the most obvious and natural human response is to try to avoid it at all costs. Of course you want to run away from it. Why wouldn't you? You might try to distract yourself as much as possible from what's upsetting you. And there's a million ways to do that. Shopping, alcohol, eating, being busy. You might try to ignore it. Cover up your "negative" emotions to make yourself feel better. That might work in the short term but those emotions will come back to haunt you later. Trust me on this. Being able to make peace with your emotions and just sit with them takes courage. It's a huge part of self-mastery and building resilience.

> *"If you are playing the game without wounds, you are not playing the game, you are watching the game. If you are*

192

A few years ago when my father died, I learned a big lesson about myself and how I handle uncomfortable emotional situations. And because of that awareness, I've since seen it in others on multiple occasions. I went into Superwoman mode. Daddy was in a care home and they needed me to clear the room within the week. Within *a day*, I was on it. Hiring a van. Getting all his stuff out of the home. Packing it all up. Sorting everything into charity bags and things I'd keep. I was a woman on a super-organised mission. I'd do *anything* but just sit and come to terms with what had just happened. I was possessed with getting everything "done" and massively distracting myself in any way possible.

Actionable advice

So what should I have done instead? Felt it. Sat with those emotions so they could come up and be felt. Emotions are like letters you receive in the post with messages attached. They come to deliver a message and you need to be able to receive those messages rather than "not being in". They need to be felt so they can be processed. I did eventually take time to process the grief and sit with the emotions. But, I could have done it *much* sooner.

> "We cannot selectively numb emotions. When we numb the painful emotions, we also numb the positive emotions."
> **BRENÉ BROWN, PROFESSOR, RESEARCHER AND AUTHOR**

Distraction is a tool we all employ a lot of the time. Particularly when something really horrible happens. People decide to go back to work "to take their minds off it" when someone dies, which is totally understandable. But there needs to be a real balance here between getting on with life and getting *so **distracted*** that you don't actually make the time to process what's just happened. Because it's painful. But remember, emotions need to be felt. And that requires attention, not distraction.

ACTION/CONSIDERATION

Are you aware of situations where you need to process emotions?

Do you have a mechanism or a practice for doing this?

If not, what could you do to make sure you give yourself time and space?

How do you distract yourself when there's something you don't want to deal with?

What might "sitting with" discomfort look like for you?

PEARL 41

....

Choose quality over quantity

"Quality is more important than quantity.
One home run is much better than two doubles."
STEVE JOBS, BUSINESSMAN, INVENTOR
AND INVESTOR

This applies to every area of your life. From your clothes to your friendships. We talked about friendships earlier on. And I think friendship is a stellar example of the wisdom of quality over quantity.

"Keep good company, read good books, love good things and
cultivate soul and body as faithfully as you can."
LOUISA MAY ALCOTT, AMERICAN NOVELIST
AND POET

We live in a time when we've never had so much *stuff*. Things are made cheaper. And in vast quantities. And we throw them away quicker. Whether it's clothes or washing machines. Anyone over the age of 50 will trot out the phrase, "they don't make 'em like they used to". And unfortunately, it's true. Many things *aren't* built to last because we've been encouraged to just chuck them away and buy another one of whatever it is, to replace it.

But with a bit more mindfulness around the future of our planet, attitudes to buying and chucking stuff away are *slowly* shifting. And it's always good to see people using their creativity and initiative to upcycle one thing into another. I love that. I was also heartened during lockdown to hear and see so many people having monster clear-outs. Charity shops were inundated with black bin liners full of things people decided they could live without.

I remember learning the quality-versus-quantity lesson in my early twenties. I'd come home to visit my parents and went shopping with my mum in Birmingham. Now, my mum wasn't one to splash the cash around. She was careful and money-savvy. I was looking for a navy-blue blazer. A classic piece. Dress up for work, dress down with jeans. We'd been looking for a while with no luck. We were about to give up when suddenly I spotted a Hugo Boss blazer on a mannequin in quite a pricey shop window. She saw me looking at it and suggested we go in. I put it on and it fitted like a glove. When you get a piece of clothing like a blazer which sits cleanly on your shoulders and is exactly the right arm length, you know you're on to a winner. I slightly cringed when I saw the price tag. Then I heard someone say the words "buy it". My mum was telling me to buy it. Really? Careful, sensible Mum. Yep. "It's well made, classic, won't date and it'll last you for years. It may seem expensive but that's good value for money." And, boy, was she right. I wore that blazer for years and years until it virtually fell apart. And each time I wore it, I felt awesome. I had it dry-cleaned and it came up like new every time. From then on, my philosophy was to save my pennies to buy one expensive thing rather than three cheap and cheerful things. Totally worth it.

Actionable advice

What do you think about having *less* but of a *superior quality*? You may not do this with all the things you buy. I know how tempting it is to order ten items online or go and raid the big cheap clothes stores. But next time you feel tempted to go cheap and bulk, how about just pausing? How about a new strategy of quality over quantity? How much would it cost to buy *one* really well-made piece that will last you and maybe won't date?

And how about choosing to give or receive the gift of an *"experience"* rather than accumulating more possessions which need insuring, cleaning, storing and looking after. Experiences create memories and physical sensations. The exhilaration of a track day or the relaxation of spending a day at the spa, a balloon ride or a dinner will stay with you in your life's memory bank. After all, just how many handbags and pairs of shoes do you really need? *Ouch.*

ACTION/CONSIDERATION

In which aspects of your life could you adopt a "quality over quantity" approach?

How would you go about doing this?

What changes would you need to make?

What habits might you need to build or break?

PEARL 42

....

Create space in your life

> *"Decluttering is infinitely easier when you think of it as deciding what to keep, rather than deciding what to throw away."*
>
> **FRANCINE JAY, MINIMALIST AND DECLUTTERING EXPERT**

And talking of having a good clear-out, letting go of stuff is immensely empowering. Whether you're letting go of relationships that no longer serve you, beliefs that no longer serve you or stuff you no longer use or wear. Letting go releases energy and creates *space*.

My parents' generation, who grew up with rationing during the war, were loathe to throw anything away. Which is kind of understandable. Nowadays, for *most* of us, we're lucky enough not to have that hanging over us. It's more about saving waste and recycling. So ask yourself – do you keep stuff you simply don't use, need or want? Do you sense that at "some point in the future" it just *might* be useful?

So WTF is all *that* about?

We're back to attachment. Fear. Fear of letting go. What's the worst that could happen if you passed on that dress you haven't worn in five years? That you've kept just in case it comes back into fashion? Just in case. Hanging on is an energy of fear. Are you holding on to the past? Do those clothes represent a relationship or a time in your life that you haven't actually properly said goodbye to yet? Just saying.

Austerity is a reality. Upcycle it, repurpose it, make it work. But don't have it sitting redundant in a corner waiting for "some point in the future". Donate it to charity. Let someone else have a go at giving it a new lease of life. I have a two-year rule for clothes. If two winters and two summers have passed and I haven't worn a piece of clothing, it goes in the black bin liner. Brutal, but it makes room for the new. And every so often, every cupboard, drawer, wardrobe and shelf gets put under the microscope. A cardboard box for the stuff and a black bin liner for the clothes. Off to the charity shop or a visit to e-Bay or Vinted.

I once helped a friend make a start on clearing out her multiple wardrobes. The task was really stressing her out so I suggested we take a Sunday morning and just blitz it, then have a big fat Sunday roast lunch to reward her for her efforts. I sat on her bed with a large mug of tea and multiple bags and bin liners. I got her to take everything out piece by piece. She'd got so many clothes packed so tightly in her wardrobes she couldn't see what she'd actually got. Each piece was put under the microscope. I asked her, "When did you last wear it?" and "Do you love it?" To start with, she was a little hesitant but my brutality started to become infectious and after about half an hour she was chucking stuff out with gay abandon. A few select items to sell to a vintage shop, but most of it to charity and the odd torn or faded T-shirt just went in the bin. After an hour, she put everything back in order – all the same items together and my OCD even got her to put the same colours together. She could finally see what she'd got and the wardrobe door could finally shut! The relief she felt was palpable. Space at last. We put a date in the diary to attack her other wardrobes but she felt a lot better about the whole process and wasn't so intimidated by the task. Even just asking those two simple questions helped her focus a little bit more.

Once you realise that everything in the universe is made of energy and energy needs to flow, doesn't it make total sense to set up your home and workspace so it can do precisely that? That's part of what feng shui is all about. Have you ever had a really good sort out of a room or a space? Cleared out a ton of stuff and then given it a really good clean? Doesn't it simply *feel* better? I can sense the energetic shift in a room after a good clear-out and a good clean. It's like it can breathe again. The space gives an energetic sigh of relief. And clutter isn't purely confined to clearing out stuff. Creating space in your personal life is important but it's also absolutely essential in your professional life.

If your diary is jammed day after day, month after month, it's not good for your physical or your mental health. How productive are you when this is what your working life looks like, day in, day out? Your brain is overloaded and the lack of space can lead to a feeling of overwhelm. Which in turn makes you feel like you're *reacting* to events rather than being in control of things. Sometimes taking time out to just reset and think about what your priorities actually are can help you to refocus. And rarely does anything creative and innovative come from agitated and anxious people. If you're in a state of anxiety that's fuelled by cortisol and adrenalin, this isn't a productive state for you to think clearly, make good decisions or be creative.

> *"No problem can be solved from the same level of consciousness that created it."*
> **ALBERT EINSTEIN, THEORETICAL PHYSICIST**

Actionable advice

Post-Covid, with a huge increase in working from home, it seems to have become the norm in a lot of organisations to book in meetings with no breaks in between. *Some* companies have started scheduling meetings at ten past the hour or half hour to factor some space in. This should be the rule rather than the exception as I've seen a massive rise in my clients having back-to-back meetings for much of their day. I've always been a big believer in taking a pause between meetings. If you can, are you able to put a metaphorical "full stop" at the end of one meeting before you start another? Just to take a little time to digest, reflect, or make a mental summary or a physical note of your activity and outcomes before diving headlong into the next meeting. Which is highly likely to be with an entirely different audience with a different agenda. Not even getting the chance to think about how you approach the next thing in your day or what your intention might be seems a little crazy to me.

If you want to come up with fresh new ideas, you need to create space which encourages reflection and considered thinking. Hence the "off-site" to get people away from their normal working environments. But off-sites are expensive and time-consuming, so how can you create the space you need in your working week?

I'd encourage you to carve out some space in your week where you can just *think*. About anything. About what you're doing and how you could do things differently or better. Take time to plan and reflect. Time to think strategically if you need to. It's often when you get off the hamster wheel that you have your most inspired ideas. If you control your diary, block out some time where you don't have meetings. Even if it's just making sure you take an hour for lunch when you're working from home. If you have a PA or an assistant, be explicit with them that your diary needs space. Make sure they're not booking you up beyond your realistic capacity. Please do this for your mental and physical well-being. And of course ask yourself do you actually *need* to be at every meeting that's scheduled in your diary? Maybe yes. But don't be afraid to push back or question it if people are adding you in gratuitously to meetings that you don't need to attend.

ACTION/CONSIDERATION

Do you keep stuff you know you should get rid of?

Can you put your finger on why you hang on to these things?

What's your Resistance?

How could you start managing your diary better to create space in your day?

Is there anyone you need to enlist in helping to achieve this?

PEARL 43

Wisdom for work: accept you're a brand

> *"The things that make me different*
> *are the things that make me, me."*
> **"PIGLET" – A.A. MILNE, WRITER AND POET**

We talked earlier about you following, accepting and embracing your True Nature. And this applies more than ever when you show up for work. No one else has your exact blend of personality, strengths, superpowers, experiences, skills and values. We all have a "craft" or a "tendency" towards something. Everyone has a natural affinity for something. There's a place for you to fill, that no-one else can fill. I've seen, over the years, how important it is to make sure your uniqueness doesn't go unrecognised at work, but a lot of people really struggle with this idea.

When I mention the words "Personal Brand" to my British clients, the reaction is often the same. "I *hate* thinking about myself as a product or brand." "It feels crass." "It doesn't come naturally to big myself up in that kind of way. I know I need to – but it just feels so cringey." "It all sounds very contrived." "It's just not me."

Selling oneself is so frightfully un-British. But you live in a competitive world and this is just about you being smart and taking control of your destiny. If you're remotely ambitious, you'll need to be an active player in managing your career rather than passively leaving opportunities to chance.

Actionable advice

When you're writing a CV or an online bio, when you've got a job interview or a promotion opportunity, or when you're told you need to "raise your profile", this is all about your brand. Brand is simply about being more *conscious* about how you want people to view you. What do you want them to say about you when you're not around? You want people to *get* you. And here's the thing. You take yourself for granted. We all do. Because you've lived with yourself for all these years, you take your strengths for granted. You most likely get on with your job without ever thinking *why* you're good at it, why you like it or actually what you *do* every day. And that's why going through a process of becoming more conscious of your unique abilities, strengths and value is so important. It may even make you realise you're in the *wrong* job.

To me, your Personal Brand is less about *building* anything and more about *uncovering* who you already are. And believe me when I say, it really *doesn't* have to be a cringe. The first step is to get clear on three things.

Firstly, you need to list out your assets or what I call your "basket of goodies". These are your God-given strengths and innate talents. Your superpowers. This is the stuff that comes naturally to you. Then you've got the skills you've picked up along the way. Think of all those courses you've been on and what you've learned on the job. What couldn't you do when you started your job that you can do now? And it's also about thinking about the life experiences you've had. Both the good and the bad. Running marathons can provide you with huge amounts of self-discipline. Several of my female clients have survived breast cancer and have developed huge resilience and a different outlook on life because of it. All of these experiences shape you in some way. They make you who you are today. Type it all up or write it down. Ask friends, family, trusted current and ex-colleagues, any mentors you may have had, clients past and present, to give you feedback. Others will see things in you that you don't see in yourself. And remember, this is about your strengths, talents and abilities not your development areas.

Secondly, you have your core values. What's important to you? What do you care about? What's non-negotiable to you? Values are a big part of your brand. Delivering on promises, working collaboratively, seeing things through to finish, creating a great client experience, being authentic, working in a culture of trust, integrity, honesty. These are a few of the kinds of things people talk about. I often find a good way of uncovering someone's values is to ask them what really pisses them off. This can give you a great insight into what's important to you. If people not doing what they say they're going to do sends you into orbit, what does that tell you about your value system? Perhaps dependability and reliability are real core values for you.

The third aspect of your brand is your visual image. I spend less time talking to clients about this nowadays as the world has become a far more casual and accepting place in terms of dress code. However, I still think it's worth a mention. We make snap decisions on people's capabilities, class, affluence and even sexuality in a matter of seconds on first meeting. You just want to make sure your appearance is consistent with what you want to project. Whatever that may be.

Once you've gone through the process of writing down all your assets and values and getting feedback from others, you'll start to see a pattern emerging. These consistent themes are your core brand characteristics. There'll probably be around four or five strengths, attributes, talents which people associate with you and which you will feel yourself.

The second part is getting clear on *who* you want to get your brand in front of. Then you can work on the *how*. Who is your "audience"? It could be one person like your boss or it could be a group of people like a senior leadership team. Use opportunities that crop up naturally, or even create an opportunity to get in front of your audience. I've helped clients think about how they can get on a leadership team call to showcase some of the work they're doing. The key is how you *frame* it. How you position *why* you want this opportunity to get in front of your audience. And then it's about how you play that out. It could be a face-to-face meeting, a call, an update or speaker slot at a senior leadership forum or getting involved in extracurricular activities that raise people's awareness of you. For example, some of my clients get involved in diversity and inclusion initiatives which raise their brand awareness across their wider business. It could be about using your skills, like writing, for example, to create something of value to your business or your clients.

And you know what? My client who said, "It's just not me," really appreciated the process by the end of it. It set her up to approach a recent promotion opportunity from a completely different angle. She was far more powerful. I had a major mother hen moment when I recently heard her say, "…Because I have a flair for dealing with people." She'd never have said that before. She now had the confidence to talk about herself in an entirely different way. But a way that felt authentic and right for her. And so can you.

> *"Know your worth, hold your own power, be you."*
> **MORGAN HARPER NICHOLS, MUSICIAN,**
> **WRITER AND ARTIST**

If you've got an interview, you've got to be clear on what *you* bring to the role, to the team, to the organisation. Why should they hire you and not the next person they interview? Why are you valuable? Useful? If *you're* not clear, it's going to be hard for your audience to be. I want you to feel proud of who you are, what you've achieved and what you can offer.

ACTION/CONSIDERATION

What are the thoughts and feelings that come up for you when you think about yourself as a brand?

Can you see where it could be useful to be able to articulate "why you"?

Who are your "audiences" at work who you need to influence?

Can you think of an upcoming opportunity to showcase your brand, however small you might need to start?

PEARL 44

Wisdom for work: stake your claim

> *"Behold the turtle: he only makes progress when he sticks his neck out."*
> **JAMES BRYANT CONANT, CHEMIST AND GOVERNMENT OFFICIAL**

It's 1992. Bill ("I did not have sexual relations with that woman") Clinton is elected into the White House; Barcelona hosts the Olympics and the poor Queen has her year from hell. You may have been a twinkle in your dad's eye, a teenager or a proper grown-up, but I was in my mid-twenties, gadding about the City of London, working for a posh headhunting firm, drinking champagne and thinking I was cool.

My euphoria reached new heights when the firm announced they were taking us all off for a thinly disguised tax-deductible "off-site" meeting. Aka a skiing weekend in France with a quickie strategy session thrown in to keep the taxman happy. YAY.

211

Sadly, that most joyous of tax loopholes has long since closed but let me tell you, it was glorious while it lasted. Little did I know, that little strategy session, would change my life in so many ways. During said session, the firm shared their plans to open their first overseas office in Hong Kong and announced they'd be sending people from the London office.

Honestly, you should have seen me. Hong Kong? I could barely contain myself. I was like a five-year-old who knows the answer to teacher's question. Inside my head, my hand shot up and I silently yelled, "ME, ME, pick ME, I'm the best, I can go." But, they were only going to send two people out to open the office. A senior consultant and *one* researcher.

After everyone had strategised and satisfied the taxman, I found myself in the back of a taxi en route to a restaurant in the French Alps, sitting next to the founder of the firm. Head honcho. Chief decision-maker. To be honest, I'd never had much to do with him. And I didn't have a fat lot in common with him either. I hadn't gone to public school, I didn't ride or play polo and there wasn't much pheasant shooting going on in Birmingham where I grew up.

I remember very clearly thinking one thing. Only one researcher goes to Hong Kong. It HAD to be me. Time to make my intentions clear. I rehearsed the pitch in my head. If indeed they were going to open an office in Hong Kong, I'd like to be the researcher they sent. I was experienced, I was ready for a challenge, I had no ties. I was up for it. Cue: the closest thing to a cheeky smile I thought I could get away with, without looking ridiculous.

They sent me to Hong Kong.

Seven months later, I moved out there for two and a half years and had a bloody ball. Hong Kong at that time was a bit of an ex-pat playground. I worked hard, played hard, travelled all over the region, made life-long friendships and enough money to trade up my London flat when I came home.

Now you might argue they'd have sent me anyway. Even if I'd kept my mouth shut. Yes, I was the most experienced researcher at the time. And yes, I had no ties. But, the little Pearl of Wisdom here is remarkably simple.

Stake your claim.

Actionable advice

People aren't mindreaders. Get in there first and ask for what you want. It could be anything that grabs you. Certain types of projects, certain types of clients, in different sectors or markets. Or you might want to join a different team or move to a different location. Whatever it is you want, you need to tell the right people. Nothing might come of it straight away but if you don't plant the seed, you're leaving it to chance. Yes, go with the flow and allow events to unfold. Absolutely. But make your wishes known. Get those seeds planted, first to yourself and then to the world. Then sit back and allow the Universal Mind to work its magic.

Think about how to initiate conversations and take ownership of your development and your destiny. Think carefully about how you frame that conversation. Jot some notes down or say it out loud first to make sure you sound persuasive. You can't beat a bit of role-play to find the right words. Take the emotion out of it and stick to the logical facts. And remember, some opportunities might not currently exist. So don't be afraid to be creative and suggest new opportunities or ideas you've had. Stake your claim.

> *"A woman with a voice is by definition a strong woman.*
> *But the search to find that voice can be*
> *remarkably difficult."*
> **MELINDA GATES, PHILANTHROPIST**

And, if you're struggling with kicking your own ass into gear or you feel you've plateaued or lost your way or just need to focus more on your own development needs, then go get yourself a mentor. Someone who can act as your guide, coach, advisor or consultant. Just as you're reading this book, you're taking advantage of all my years of accumulated experience, failures, fuck-ups, observations and achievements.

Some organisations have mentor programmes and will actively encourage and help you find a mentor. Sadly, these companies are the exception rather than the rule and it's often only the larger corporates who offer a mentor system. The important thing is for you to be paired with someone that's going to "work" for you rather than a random selection made by an HR person who doesn't know you from a bar of soap. The responsibility to proactively seek someone out rests firmly on your shoulders.

> *"If you cannot see where you are going,*
> *ask someone who has been there before."*
> **J LOREN NORRIS, LEADERSHIP SPEAKER**

It might be someone within your organisation who has trod a similar path to you. It might be someone you get on particularly well with who's a little more senior than you. Or, it might be someone outside your organisation. My advice is aim high, don't be afraid to ask a really senior person in your organisation or another company. Genuinely talented senior executives will often enjoy the process of "putting something back" by mentoring up-and-coming future talent. And if they can't help you, they might be able to find someone who can.

Wherever you go searching for a mentor, there are three things I want you to bear in mind: chemistry, trust and respect. You have to feel comfortable and safe talking to a mentor. You must feel that there won't be any breaches of confidentiality. No negative repercussions of you bearing your soul to them. You've also got to respect them. You need to believe that they've genuinely got something to offer you.

Before you make your approach, stop and ask yourself what you want from the mentoring process. Get clear about your intention, your Why. Think about the frequency, location and timing of your sessions. What works for you and what works for them? And make sure you're honest about how it's going. Having the odd feedback session as part of the process is vital. A mentoring process is likely to be a bit "suck it and see" for both of you to start with.

Having someone you can trust (in confidence) to talk through challenges you have at work is invaluable. Some people work with a coach, some people have both a mentor and a coach. But a lot of people don't even think to ask for one, let alone seek one out. Odds are, if you don't ask, you won't get.

ACTION/CONSIDERATION

What do you want? Really want?

Have you thought about how and when to ask? Who needs to hear it?

Is there a conversation you could have about any opportunities at work?

Do you think you need help?

What issues or challenges might be useful to discuss with a mentor?

Who might your ideal mentor be and how might you find or approach them?

PEARL 45

....

Wisdom for work: stay current

"Knowledge is power."

FRANCIS BACON, IRISH BRITISH PAINTER

There are a couple of other things I'd suggest you bear in mind when thinking about proactively managing your career. Firstly, I'd strongly recommend that you're always aware of your current market value. Forgive me if that makes you feel like a commodity or a property. But, as an ex-headhunter, I know how important it is that you're in touch with this aspect of your job. How is your role or a similar one paid at your competitor organisations? When you come to have discussions about promotions and pay rises, it's important you've done your homework and you know your worth. Remember, knowledge is power. Somewhere in your network you need a good-quality recruiter or headhunter who you can ask for advice on compensation levels. If you don't have one, I strongly recommend you seek one out. If you've been approached by a recruiter for a role you didn't want, maybe go back and have a chat.

Secondly, it's a good idea to keep your CV or online profile updated. In the spirit of *"do it when you can rather than when you have to"*, it might be an idea to dust it off and have a look. Or create one if you haven't got one already. Just so when that job opportunity you're interested in comes along, you don't have the huge task of creating something from scratch. That could feel overwhelming and time pressured. You want to be able to take time to reflect on your achievements and experience and think about your brand. Also, because you're doing your job day in day out, you forget all the stuff you've done. The skills you've built, the courses you've been on, qualifications you've gained, the projects you've completed, the business you've won, the events you've spoken at, the panels you've been on, the people you've trained, all the achievements you've accomplished, both large and small. Internal and external. There are two questions I'd ask you to see how you've developed both personally and professionally. How are *you* different now versus when you started your role? How is your *role* different from when you started? What's been the impact of that?

ACTION/CONSIDERATION

Do you have a CV or online profile?

When was the last time you looked at it?

What needs updating?

Are you aware of your market worth?

Who could you talk to or stay in touch with to keep this current?

PEARL 46

....

Wisdom for work: learn to communicate concisely

> *"I have only made this letter longer because I have not had the time to make it shorter."*
> **BLAISE PASCAL, PHILOSOPHER, LETTER 16,**
> **THE PROVINCIAL LETTERS**

Take it from me, if there's one skill that will stand you in good stead throughout your whole life, let alone your career, it's this. If you can learn to *be concise,* it'll serve you well. And it's never too late. I've lost count of the times I've sat in meetings, presentations or on telephone calls thinking, "will you get to the bloody point?"

Being succinct can be difficult because you actually need to think far more carefully about what you're trying to say. You need to filter stuff *out*. It's much easier to overload the conversation, the meeting, the e-mail, the presentation, the pitch, with everything you know about a subject. It's a lot harder to include just the absolute must-haves.

I think there's several reasons why people can't be concise. If you know too much about your subject, that can be dangerous. People who are subject-matter experts are often guilty of pitching and presenting *way* too much information. Remember, you always need to put yourself in your audience's shoes, whatever the situation. Don't fall into the trap of trying to justify your existence. Some people think that the more they say, the more credible they'll appear. Well let me tell you, that's bullshit. The inability to get to the point is hugely frustrating for any audience. It can really affect how people perceive you. And it can damage your brand.

And you know, I actually think that the other reason people aren't concise is *fear*. Fear of leaving something out, fear of not appearing knowledgeable enough. When you can let go of the need to justify, you'll master the art of being concise. If you're doing a presentation, be brave enough to leave some of your content for the Q&A.

Actionable advice

One of the biggest mistakes people make is giving too much context and background information up front. Limit this to what's absolutely necessary to get everyone up to speed, *and no more*.

Something else you might also want to try if you don't already know about it, is the tried-and-tested "Power of Three". I say tried and tested because it's been around a long time. Three is a magic number. Successful books, films, plays and presentations are often written in a three-act format. Presidents Kennedy and Obama built most of their speeches on the rule of three. Steve Jobs used this format in all his Apple presentations.* Once you start being conscious, you'll see the Power of Three all around you.

The Power of Three is also invaluable for the unexpected. If you're asked to contribute in a meeting or to present your thoughts on something out of the blue, don't panic. Just ask yourself, "what three things do they absolutely need to know?" It's simple but it really helps focus your thinking. It's also great if you're under time pressure. If you're crystal clear on your Power of Three, it's a whole load easier to know what to say.

The other thing I've noticed over the years is that people will start to talk or answer a question before they actually know what they're going to say. So the first few sentences or paragraphs are just a load of unnecessary waffle. Try pausing before you speak to allow your brain to get its act together before you open your mouth! And then just focus on what three *specific* things you want your audience to remember. Stick to that and don't overload the content. If you're not clear on what your three key messages are, your audience won't stand a chance.

ACTION/CONSIDERATION

Are you aware that sometimes you waffle or say too much?

Why do you think that is? Nerves? Justification? Fear of not saying everything?

Which aspects of your communications in both your professional and personal life can you focus on using the Power of Three to be more concise?

What's the first opportunity you might have to practise this?

PEARL 47

·····························

Wisdom for work: learn to engage audiences confidently

> *"All the great speakers were bad speakers at first."*
> **RALPH WALDO EMERSON, POET AND AUTHOR**

One of the most stressful and anxiety-provoking situations in life is having to stand up and present in front of others. It's most people's idea of hell. But it's vitally important, because if you can become a more confident presenter, it's going to help you in other areas of your life. Just knowing that if you had to, you could stand up and speak in front of others without turning into a jabbering wreck gives a great sense of inner strength and confidence. In most jobs, at some point you'll need to stand up and speak in front of others, so getting better at it rather than putting it off is a smart strategy.

So here's my "Presenting 101" so you can really nail this crucial life skill. I've spent the last twenty-five years helping many hundreds of clients conquer their fear of public speaking. From multi-million-pound pension fund pitches to best man and groom speeches and funeral eulogies and everything in between. Follow this guidance and I promise you'll feel a whole load better about it – but like any skill, you need to practise if you're going to improve.

Actionable advice

The first thing to remember is that there's a huge difference between talking ***with*** someone and talking ***at*** someone. You know what it's like when someone talks ***at*** you. It's bloody boring, for a start. It's the same when you're presenting. You need to create a sense of intimacy, connection and engagement with your audience. Even very large groups. And there are a number of ways you can do that.

To create great engagement with any audience, you need to involve them wherever you can. You need to make your content as directly relevant to your audience as possible. Be very clear on *why* they should care about what you're saying. What's the impact on them? What are the consequences or benefits for them? Ask yourself what's the *So What?* for my audience. Ask them questions, get them to think about or imagine scenarios in their heads, based on their own personal experiences which are directly relevant to what you're talking about. Use phrases like "I'd like you to imagine" or "Picture this". Get them to put their hands up in response to a question. Just get them *involved*.

To engage with any audience, you need to look at them. Now I know that might sound bloody obvious but you'd be amazed at how many people don't. Not everyone's comfortable with eye contact, but it's vital to build connection with your audience. And if you know this is something you find hard, I suggest you start practising it in more informal situations. Just hold your gaze for a fraction of a second longer and make an effort to look people in the eye. It makes you look a lot more confident, even if you're not feeling it.

And get as physically close to your audience as you can. Take away any barriers. If my clients are speaking at a conference, I always encourage them to get out from behind the lectern so they can walk freely round the stage and get closer to the audience. Years ago, I watched a televised US presidential debate between George Bush Senior and the then-senator Bill Clinton. Check it out on YouTube,* it's an absolute slam-dunk masterclass in what we're talking about here. A woman in the audience asked both candidates quite a personal question about how the poor state of the economy was affecting them personally. Bush Senior stayed on his stool on the stage and semi-answered the question but not in a hugely satisfactory way. He wasn't the most charismatic of men.

Clinton, however, got off his stool and walked right to the edge of the stage so he was as close to the woman as he could possibly get. He then repeated the question to make sure he'd fully understood it. The game-changer was the way he gave her his full present-centred attention during his whole answer. And he could only do that because he was about ten feet away from her, looking directly into her eyes. You could tell by the woman's expression she was putty in his hands. Mr Charisma. If you talk in a conversational way using key words or short bullet points to remind you what to say rather than writing out full scripted sentences, it'll stop you sounding like a robot. Also avoid using jargon, corporatese or three-letter acronyms which your audience might not understand.

The more the connection, the more fulfilling and satisfying you'll find it. You might still be nervous, but you're less likely to show it. There's nothing worse than standing in front of a group, reading off a script or a bunch of PowerPoint slides and feeling like you're boring everyone to death because it's a one-way monologue. If you change the dynamic and start making it interactive, you'll create a totally different vibe.

And, if you remember the Power of Three, this will help you limit the amount of content you put together. What are the three things you absolutely want your audience to remember? Then structure your presentation around these.

A big part of feeling more confident standing up in front of others is feeling physically comfortable and relaxed. Taking a grounded, solid stance with legs hip width apart, so you're feeling planted, is a good start. Many women I coach cross one leg in front of the other when they stand to present. Apart from making them look like they need to pee (always go before), they look unbalanced and unsure of themselves. If you want to move around, that's great, but always come back to that planted stance. And if you're a naturally expressive person then yes use your hands, it's part of how you communicate. Just take all the distractions away. Coins in pockets, clicking pens, tie your hair back and take rings off if you know you're a fiddler. Then you can stop obsessing about what's going on with your own body and focus all of your attention on your audience.

And I've saved the most powerful tool for last.

For as long as I can remember, I've been teaching my clients to master the use of the pause when they present. And I'm not exaggerating when I say it's been an absolute game changer for hundreds of them. Is it simple? Yes. Is it easy? Hell, not always. Humans are naturally uncomfortable with silence. So, if you can master this, you'll have gained a super-skill. And not just in presenting. You'll find it useful in all sorts of situations, both at home and at work. Remember when we talked earlier about saying No to something and pausing afterwards for impact? This is it.

After you've delivered a key message, an important statistic or fact, a rhetorical question – just stop. For two or three seconds. Like you're saying to your audience, "have you got that?" It might feel like forever but trust me, it's not (video yourself if you don't believe me). It gives your audience the time to think about what you've said and to engage with it. It also buys you time to breathe, have a sip of water, look at your notes, and makes you come across as relaxed, unhurried and super confident. If you can combine the pause with your eye contact, it will take your impact to the next level.

You can also pause *before* you speak. A lot of people use fillers like "um" or "er" which is fine *occasionally*. But it can become distracting if you do it too much. By using a pause before you speak, you give yourself time to look at your bullet points and *think* about how you're going to say your next point. The more you pause, both before and after you speak, the more confident you'll look and feel.

I guarantee if you use and practise these tools, they will help you enormously. Just like they have helped hundreds of my clients before you. Maybe start by using some of these tips in more informal everyday situations. For example, practise using the pause in normal conversations or in meetings just to get used to it. Like building any habit, it requires repetition.

ACTION/CONSIDERATION

How do you feel about speaking in public?

If you got better at it could it help advance your career or your brand?

What might be a low-risk opportunity to start practising some of these tools?

Which of the tools resonated the most with you?

Can you find a regular opportunity to practise these skills?

PEARL 48

....

Wisdom for work: learn to manage feedback

> *"We all need people who will give us feedback.*
> *That's how we improve."*
> **BILL GATES, BUSINESSMAN, INVENTOR,**
> **PHILANTHROPIST AND WRITER**

I know it sounds obvious but it's really important that you understand how you're doing at work. So rather than waiting for the once- or twice-yearly appraisal, I'm going to suggest you take matters into your own hands. Ask for feedback more regularly.

And the reason I'm suggesting you *ask* for it – is that a lot of people, including some very senior people, really suck at giving feedback. There are many reasons why people don't give feedback or helpful feedback. Sometimes it's because they feel uncomfortable giving you what you might take as "negative" or critical comments. They're worried about offending you or the impact it's going to have. Sometimes they don't know how to frame it. And sometimes they're just too busy. It doesn't occur to them to do it. Giving you feedback isn't high on their list of priorities. So you need to remind them.

And let's face it, companies have varying standards of performance feedback systems. Some I've seen are pretty good. A lot are crap and just pay lip service to it. Often, a good appraisal system can be spoilt by a manager who can't be bothered to do a proper job. Or by someone who's so busy that they don't prepare, it gets rushed and then isn't useful. And by the way, if you *do* manage people, there's nothing more demotivating and counterproductive for an employee than a poorly executed appraisal. Just saying.

Actionable advice

This simple tool was passed on to me by my coach, David. It makes it so much easier for you to ask for feedback and to get a better-quality response. Just ask for three things that you did or do well, and one stretch. The 3:1 tool. Back to the Power of Three. So, if there's *one thing* for you to work on, what is it? This can be used for specific events – like a pitch or a presentation or a project or it can be used for ongoing general job performance. What three things are you currently doing well and what one thing needs more of your attention and focus?

The other thing I come across a lot is a manager or team leader giving broad, generic feedback. If someone tells you that you need to "be more confident", or "be more professional", what the hell does that mean? This kind of feedback is deeply unhelpful and doesn't move you on at all. What *specifically* do they want you to do differently? What behaviours are they looking for? What does "be more professional" mean? Stop walking round the office with no shoes on? Stop turning up late to meetings? Address a lack of attention to detail? What?

One reason managers can be reluctant to give feedback is if they think you're going to get defensive. This is important because it can damage your career prospects. It makes people wary because they don't feel they can be straight with you. "Treading on eggshells" is an expression I hear a lot. And it can be a real blocker.

> *"If you are irritated by every rub,*
> *how will your mirror be polished?"*
> **RUMI, SUFI MYSTIC AND POET**

Just put aside the temptation to be offended and listen to what's being said in the spirit of being open-minded. I suggest you ask for recent examples so you can understand the feedback more clearly. If the person *can't* give you examples, there might be a couple of reasons for that. Either it's just *their perception* or a feeling they're getting with no real evidence. OR it's an uncomfortable subject and they're struggling to articulate what *precisely* they want you to do differently. Make sure you hear the person out and really listen to what they're saying. If you're not sure what they're getting at, ask for more clarity so you can understand it better. You can't make changes if you're unclear on what you're being asked to do differently. I'm always surprised by the number of clients who come to me for coaching after their appraisals and are absolutely none the wiser what they've been asked to work on.

Having said that, I encourage you to have a critical filter when you're getting feedback. You don't have to *blindly* accept everything that someone says about your performance. Perhaps you feel part of it is genuinely unfair or that they simply have no evidence for what they're saying. You can accept part of it and push back on part of it. Or at least explore and discuss it more so you can unpack it and understand it.

And, if you do ever get feedback that makes you emotional, ask to take a break and just breathe and then come back. Create some distance and use that time to process. Then you can come back and *respond* rather than react. There's a big difference between a response and a reaction and it's usually a time lapse. If you stop and take a pause or a breath, you can often filter out the primeval gut reaction and turn it into a more measured response. By resisting the temptation to say the first thing that comes into your head, you can be more emotionally intelligent about how you deal with certain inflammatory situations or people. Although quick reactions are useful in some emergency situations, better outcomes usually happen in life when you respond rather than react!

> *"The best fighter is never angry."*
> **LAO TZU, ANCIENT PHILOSOPHER**

ACTION/CONSIDERATION

Where in your work could you ask for more feedback?

Would that be on a recent project or more regularly?

If you've recently had an appraisal, did you understand everything that was said and precisely what you need to work on?

If not — what do you need to do?

How might you improve your own skills when giving feedback to others?

PEARL 49

Wisdom for work: learn to manage expectations and perceptions

> *"The goal of managing upward is not to curry favour… it's about being more effective."*
> **LIZ SIMPSON, CLINICAL RESEARCH CONSULTANT, HARVARD BUSINESS SCHOOL**

Let me tell you about a conversation I had years ago with a graduate. She hadn't had any work experience, but she'd got a smart head on her shoulders. We were talking about the transition from university to work. She asked me if I had any tips on how she could be the most effective and successful in her job.

"One of the main things you'll need to do is to learn to manage upwards," I said. She looked at me as if I'd just grown another head.

"What do you mean manage *upwards?*"

"Well," I explained, "managing expectations is a key part of being in any organisation. And part of that is actually *managing your boss.*"

She still kept looking at me as if I was a complete lunatic. "I thought my boss was meant to manage *me.*"

"Well yes," I said. "But this is slightly different. A big part of your success will depend on how good you become at managing others' *expectations.* And in particular, your boss's expectations. On timelines, deliverables, your work capacity, your hours and any other number of things." She looked very puzzled.

A couple of years, later when she'd become a successful researcher in the same firm, I reminded her of our conversation and she smiled. *"God, you were right."*
Give the old girl some credit, I thought.

Actionable advice

Whatever industry you work in, it's likely you'll have some expectation management to deal with. And a lot of that might be with your boss. If you're a people pleaser, this could be challenging. If your boundaries are weak, you could end up working long hours and being overwhelmed by the volume of work or unrealistic deadlines because you're not managing expectations well enough. Giving people notice of where you're at on a project, making sure they know the timelines you're working on and what's realistic are all part of managing others' expectations. Managing upwards can also be about being proactive. Making sure your boss has the right documents for an upcoming meeting well in advance, or that you've done something that needs doing without being asked. Another element of managing expectations is telling the right people quickly when things aren't going to plan. The natural human tendency is to want to say nothing and hope it all goes away. Of course, it rarely does. Burying your head in the sand like an ostrich is the worst thing you can do. The sooner you alert people to the fact that something looks like it might be going Pete Tong the better. Then they can do something before it gets completely out of hand. The longer you leave it, the worse the situation is likely to become. So whatever happens, please *don't be an ostrich*.

Being mindful of how you're coming across in an office environment is also useful. If your workplace is open-plan, you're highly visible. So in some organisations, the way you look and what you say becomes very obvious. People can jump to conclusions about you based on the most trivial bits of behaviour. Things you may not even realise you're doing. There's something called the *horns and halo effect* that would be useful for you to be aware of. Let me explain it the best I can.

> *"People see what they want to see and what people want to see never has anything to do with the truth."*
> **ROBERTO BOLAÑO, NOVELIST, STORY-WRITER, POET AND ESSAYIST**

As humans, the way our brains work makes us judgemental and naturally hugely biased. If someone has a particular characteristic, positive or negative, we tend to form an **overall** positive or negative impression based on that one characteristic. Say, for example, you see someone as attractive. Your brain will assume that because they have this one positive characteristic, they are also positive in other areas, like being generous, smart or trustworthy. Which of course could be utter bullshit. And if you think about it the other way round – one small piece of so-called "negative behaviour" like being late for a meeting or turning up unprepared, could influence someone to judge you poorly on the **whole** of your character. Like your overall level of competence. I know this sounds crazy, unfair and irrational but it's the way our biased brains work. It's just worth bearing in mind.

ACTION/CONSIDERATION

Where could you manage expectations better at work?

What areas might this be around? Workload capacity? Hours? Deadlines?

Is there anything going on at the moment that has the potential to go off the rails and needs flagging to someone?

Are there any minor negative aspects of your behaviour that you think could be influencing others' overall perception of you? What might you do about it?

PEARL 50

....

Wisdom for work:
know your limits

"Don't sail out farther than you can row back."
DANISH PROVERB

You know I'd always be the first to encourage you to inch out of your comfort zone. But I also think it's very important for you to understand your limitations. Just so you don't get yourself into trouble. There's a difference between being courageous and being reckless. Limitations can be the amount of work you're capable of doing, the amount of stress you're under or simply the extent of your knowledge. Which is always going to have a limit, no matter how senior you become. We've obviously talked about boundaries and saying No. We've talked about managing expectations and telling the appropriate people when you feel you need help. It's just smart to recognise when you've reached your limits.

Actionable advice

Throughout my working life, I've always admired people who are aware of their limitations and aren't afraid to admit it. They seek help from others who can move them forward. So this might be the time for you to seek out that mentor we talked about. Or you might need some other kind of support. Coaching or training. We've seen it done both well and badly in politics. Smart US presidents who have surrounded themselves with highly capable individuals who are skilled where they aren't. But the reverse is also true. How many times have we seen the results of arrogant individuals who think they know better? Who don't know their limitations and think they're invincible with an out of control ego. A sure-fire recipe for disaster.

And closely linked to asking for help, is the power of asking questions at work when you're unsure of something. This might sound so bloody obvious but I can't tell you the amount of times I've seen people get themselves in a right pickle simply because they didn't ask when they weren't sure. Graduates are particularly guilty of this. "They'll think I'm stupid." "I want to show I'm smart and not ask too many questions." Actually, a lot of employers I know are far more impressed by people who ask questions than by people who don't. Of course you *can* try and work out the answer if that's possible. But don't waste a load of your precious time when one quick question would give you what you need. Work smart. Your time is your most precious commodity. The worst thing is if you don't ask, people will assume you know more than you do. And that can be dangerous. You're just kicking a problem down the road which will undoubtedly bite you on the arse at some future point. Seen it a million times. Some cultures also see it as a weakness to ask questions. But as I see it, it's the only way you're going to learn. The more questions the better. Clearly, don't keep asking the *same question* but don't shy away from asking because you feel your ego might be bruised or you might look stupid.

> "And I like asking questions, to keep learning; people with big egos might not want to look unsure."
> **HESTON BLUMENTHAL, CHEF, TV PERSONALITY AND FOOD WRITER**

ACTION/CONSIDERATION

Have you ever reached a point in a project, a piece of work or in your day to day where you felt you'd reached the limit of your capabilities?

What did you do?

What's your attitude to asking questions at work?

A final word from Sassy

So here you are. You've reached the end of the book. You've now got 50 Pearls of Wisdom to draw on whenever and wherever you need them. And, you have me, sitting on your shoulder, cheering you on. You're stuck with me now!

I hope you've had some "aha" moments along the way and some revelations about yourself or others. Perhaps you plan to build some new habits or break a few? It's an ongoing journey, this life of yours. You're never done, never finished. All I can ask is that you keep an open and curious mind and that you don't waste this precious life of yours on anything or anyone that isn't worthy of you.

Keep doing things that make you feel just a little uncomfortable, keep building that courage muscle and remember to carve out some quiet time for yourself without your distractions. Listen to your intuition and don't *ever* be afraid to ask for what you want.

If you have enjoyed it, why don't you tell your girlfriends or indeed anyone you think might benefit from these

Pearls. And keep in touch with me and the rest of the Sassy community by subscribing to my YouTube channel, following me on Instagram and subscribing to monthly Pearl Drops on the website: www.thesassygodmother.com

Go girl.

Your Sassy Godmother
X

Resources

Pearl 1 – Be your own best friend
Check out *Elephant Journal* **www.elephantjournal.com** for some good articles on maitri and practical Buddhist principles.

Pearl 3 – Live with intention
Lifebook online – go to this website and check out Lifebook
www.mindvalley.com
Created by Jon and Missy Butcher.

Pearl 4 – Discover and follow your True Nature
If you want to read a brilliant book about the Introvert/Extrovert, pick up Susan Cain's book, ***Quiet – The Power of Introverts in a World that Can't Stop Talking.***

Pearl 6 – Be aware of your programming
Bruce Lipton interview with Lynne McTaggart. His work on epigenetics is fascinating.
https://www.youtube.com/watch?v=38CBtv1-w3M

Pearl 8 – Reconnect with your feminine self

If you want to understand more about embodied movement practice, check out a lady called Jenna Ward.
https://www.jennaward.co

She offers a Primal Feminine Flow programme. These useful exercises and videos will help you start to inhabit your body and build more connection and depth with your feminine. It's not yoga or fitness, it's movement.

Pearl 12 – Catch yourself people pleasing
Courtesy of Jon Kabat-Zinn from his book of the same title.

Pearl 22 – Prioritise joy
William Bloom is one of the UK's leading educators, activists and authors in the field of holistic well-being, meditation and spiritual practice.
William Bloom https://williambloom.com

Pearl 30 – Do the tough stuff first
Delaying Gratification from *The Road Less Travelled* by M. Scott Peck.

Pearl 36 – Understand the imposter
Mind the Gap – KPMG Study of 750 high-performing senior women.

Pearl 46 – Learn to communicate concisely
MacBook Air launch – https://youtu.be/ kvfrVrh76Mk?si=ZBDec7uMWL5msq2g

For more on the Power of Three check out *The Presentation Secrets of Steve Jobs* by Carmine Gallo.

Pearl 47 – Learn to engage audiences confidently
Bill Clinton and George Bush Snr. Presidential debate
https://youtu.be/7ffbFvKlWqE?si=ouppwqy5l8hc2yt0

Suggested further reading

If you've enjoyed this book then here's my list of recommended reading for you to explore further. See what resonates with you.

The Self-Esteem Companion – Matthew McKay, PhD, Patrick Fanning, Carole Honeychurch, Catharine Sutker

Head Start: Build a Resilient Mindset So You Can Achieve Your Goals – Ian Price

Big Magic: Creative Living Beyond Fear – Elizabeth Gilbert

The Element: How Finding Your Passion Changes Everything – Ken Robinson

Flip It: How to Get the Best out of Everything – Michael Heppell

The Field – Lynne McTaggart

Power vs. Force: The Hidden Determinants of Human

Behaviour – David R. Hawkins M.D., PhD

E-Squared: Nine Do-It-Yourself Energy Experiments That Prove Your Thoughts Create Your Reality – Pam Grout

Intuition: Access Your Inner Wisdom, Trust Your Instincts, Find Your Path – Anisha Ghadiali

The Universe Has Your Back: How to Feel Safe and Trust Your Life No Matter What – Gabriella Bernstein

The Road Less Travelled – M. Scott Peck

The Power of Intention – Dr Wayne W. Dyer

The Power of Now – Eckhart Tolle

Molecules of Emotion: Why You Feel the Way You Feel – Candace B. Pert, PhD

Spiritual Activator: 5 Steps to Clearing, Unblocking and Protecting Your Energy to Attract More Love, Joy and Purpose – Oliver Niño

The Biology of Belief: Unleashing the Power of Consciousness, Matter and Miracles – Bruce H. Lipton, PhD

The Divine Matrix – Gregg Braden

The Tao of Physics: An Exploration of the Parallels Between Modern Physics and Eastern Mysticism – Fritjof Capra

Reality Is Not What It Seems: The Journey to Quantum Gravity – Carlo Rovelli

Lean In: Women, Work, and the Will to Lead – Sheryl Sandberg

The Secret Thoughts of Successful Women: Why Capable People Suffer from the Imposter Syndrome and How to Thrive in Spite of It – Valerie Young ED.D

Love Worth Making: How to Have Ridiculously Great Sex in a Long-Lasting Relationship – Stephen Snyder, M.D

Eight Dates: To Keep Your Relationship Happy, Thriving and Lasting – John Gottman and Julie Schwartz Gottman

Acknowledgements

This book wouldn't be what it is without all the wonderful clients I've worked with over the last three decades. Their openness and courage to change has been inspiring. I consider it a privilege to have worked so closely and personally with so many people who trusted me to help them.

A big part of the wisdom outlined in this book has its roots in age-old spiritual teachings. My spiritual journey began over thirty years ago and was no doubt accelerated by the wisdom and dedication to spiritual mastery of Roy Maunder. The conversations we've had during the course of our friendship have been illuminating, if not somewhat baffling at times. Not least so, when we first met and you reliably informed me, "Of course you do realise that your soul and my soul are the same." This puzzled me for many years. Until I finally got it. You are a blessing, my dear friend.

To Casey Freeman of Periwinkle PR, without whom the digital side of *Sassy Godmother* would have been an utter disaster! You have cajoled, nudged, prompted and encouraged this former tech dinosaur right from the beginning of this process. Thank you for your support, guidance and invaluable advice. You're a treasure and I wish you every success in your business. You deserve it.

To David Saville, my coach. You are an inspiration and a role model for becoming more. I wouldn't be where I am today without you and the work we did together.

And finally (there's always a "and finally", usually saved for the personal rock and support who picks up the pieces when it all goes tits, makes you a cuppa and tells you it will all work out in the end. And mine is no exception) Stevie, my Tigger, you've been a staunch supporter of Sassy from the get-go. You've believed in me and thought that what I had to say was valuable. You've supported me at every stage of the process, in every way you possibly could, and I can't thank you enough. This wouldn't have happened without you, my darling.

About the author

Susie Hall has been a coach, trainer and speaker for the last three decades, initially specialising in presentation, pitch and communication skills. She's worked globally for FT-SE listed companies, financial institutions and organisations of all shapes and sizes across a breadth of sectors from graduate to chief executive level. As The Impact Coach, she's helped thousands of clients over the years to be more confident versions of themselves, whatever situation they're in. Over the last decade, she's worked more holistically and personally with clients, helping them change their lives for the better.

She's known for being direct and challenging but always with a sense of fun and with her clients' best interests always at the heart of what she does. Sassy Godmother is Susie's alter ego. She aims to inspire a younger generation of women to be bold, courageous and outrageously authentic.

Susie splits her time between Hampshire and Buckinghamshire and looks forward to building a menagerie when the time is right.